CROSS-COUNTRY SKIING

A Complete Beginner's Book

CROSS-COUNTRY

Julian Messner

New York

SKIING A Complete Beginner's Book

by George Sullivan

Illustrated with photographs

JULIAN MESSNER and colophon are trademarks of Simon & Schuster,
registered in the U.S. Patent and Trademark Office.

Manufactured in the United States of America

Design by Virginia M. Soule'

Library of Congress Cataloging in Publication Data

Sullivan, George, 1927-
   Cross-country skiing.

   Includes index.
   SUMMARY: Discusses cross-country skiing, the
equipment, clothing, basic techniques, preparations,
and precautions. Lists places to ski and the names
of skiing guidebooks.
   1. Cross-country skiing—Juvenile literature.
2. Cross-country skiing—United States—Directories—
Juvenile literature. 3. Cross-country skiing—Canada—
Directories—Juvenile literature. [1. Cross-country
skiing. Skis and skiing] I. Title.
GV 855.3,S94   796.93   80-19798
ISBN 0-671-33098-5

Contents

PHOTO CREDITS

"There are no crowds, no noise, no confusion. You're on your own."

1 How It Began

The thermometer read 26 degrees and snow flurries swirled about as 12-year-old Scott Herrick, his younger sister, and his mother and father clamped on their special lightweight skinny skis and set out on a woodland trail. With smooth, clean strides, they glided easily over the fresh snow.

In the deep forest, all was silent. A rabbit darted across Scott's path. Once he thought he saw a fox. His father pointed out deer tracks.

The trail led over a gentle hill, and they skied fast down the other side. They crossed a frozen pond, and stopped for lunch in a big meadow on the other side. In the small pack Scott was wearing about his waist, he carried sandwiches, a candy bar, and a thermos of hot chocolate.

The Herrick family was taking part in America's fastest growing winter sport—*cross-country skiing*. It is also known as *ski touring* or *Nordic skiing*.

While the Herricks happened to be in western Massachusetts,

not far from Pittsfield, you can go cross-country skiing almost anywhere. A local park or golf course will do. You can even ski in your own backyard.

Hundreds of New Yorkers go cross-country skiing in Central Park. Tall buildings are on every side. The subway is never more than a few minutes away.

"It's fun," says Scott Herrick. "When I'm in the woods, I feel like an explorer. I see things that maybe no one's ever seen before. And it's easy. It's just like walking."

Skiing In Early Times

Although cross-country skiing is one of the newer American sports, it is actually many centuries old. Exactly how old, nobody

Cross-country skiing in New York's Central Park.

knows for sure. But not many years ago, archaeologists unearthed a crude ski in a Swedish peat bog, and it was found to be 5,000 years old. Rock carvings depicting skiing have been found in caves in Norway and on the shores of the White Sea and Lake Onega in Russia.

Skiing in ancient times had nothing to do with recreation. Skis were used to help man move about on snow-covered or frozen ground. Huntsmen wore them when looking for game, chiefly reindeer and elk. Warriors used skis in battle.

Ancient skis did not look like the long, sleek runners in use today. The first skis were probably the bones of large animals.

Later, skis were split from the outer curves of tree trunks and smoothed down on one side. They were much wider and shorter than today's skis. Pine and spruce were the woods most favored. These skis were strapped to the feet by narrow strips of leather. Sometimes grooves would be hollowed out of the wood, just big enough to hold the foot in position.

During the eleventh century, some skiers decided they could increase their over-the-snow speed by making their skis of unequal length. The "kicking ski," worn on the right foot, was the shorter of the two. The "running ski," on the left foot, was longer and smoother.

Early skiers also learned the advantage of using a long stick to push themselves along. It was simply a sturdy branch, sometimes with a bone point.

SKIING AS A SPORT

Skiing as a sport is believed to date back to 1767. In that year

11

in Oslo (then known as Christiania), Norwegian soldiers competed in downhill races. The rules explained that they had to speed down the slopes "without breaking their skis or falling."

During the next century, downhill races were conducted in many parts of Europe. In the late 1850s, the royal family of Norway took note of ski jumping as a sport, awarding a trophy to the country's best jumper.

It is not known who brought the first pair of skis to North America. But skiing may have predated the first colonists. After all, Indians in Canada had used *snowshoes* for many generations. They probably made special types of snowshoes for going down steep mountain slopes, snowshoes that resembled skis in their ability to slide easily over snow.

Scandinavian immigrants introduced skiing to many parts of North America. During the rush to the Pacific Coast for gold in

A family ski outing of long ago. Note the way the children traveled.

the 1850s, skis were used in the Sierra Nevada range of California for gathering firewood and other light transportation chores.

The first cross-country skier to become well known was John A. (Snowshoe) Thomson, a native of Norway, who carried the United States mail over the snow-clad Sierras. Thomson's route covered the 91 miles between Placerville, California, and Carson City, Nevada. He carried a pack weighing 100 pounds both ways. Each round trip took a week. His salary was $200 a month. In the 20 years he carried the mail, the fearsome storms and mountainous drifts never once prevented him from keeping to his schedule.

After his retirement, he filed a claim for $6,000 which he said the government owed him. Congress sent him a letter of thanks, but no money. In Thomson's honor, a cross-country race is now held over the route he took.

One of the most courageous cross-country treks in history occurred in 1888, when Fridtjof Nansen, the Norwegian explorer, crossed the frozen wastes of Greenland on skis. In an account of his feat, Nansen wrote, "Nothing hardens the muscles and makes the body so strong and elastic; nothing steels the will-power and freshens the mind as ski-ing."

During the 1880s, skiing began to develop as a sport in the United States. Ski clubs were organized and ski-jumping contests were held.

In 1904, officials of a number of midwest ski clubs founded the National Ski Association. The name of the organization was later changed to the *United States Ski Association*. Today, USSA is recognized as the governing body of the sport.

Recreational skiing got a big boost in 1932, when the Winter Olympics were held at Lake Placid, New York. (The Olympics were held at Lake Placid again in 1980.) Thousands who attended the events returned home determined to take up skiing in one form or another. In the years that followed, scores of ski resorts were founded. Ski schools were opened almost everywhere.

After World War II, skiing became a major American sport. But the postwar boom in skiing concerned only *downhill skiing*, sometimes called *Alpine skiing*, not cross-country.

There were a few cross-country enthusiasts, but they were located in the northeast. And they were looked upon with curiosity by downhill skiers.

The situation began to change in the 1960s. Downhill ski resorts were becoming overcrowded. Skiers were spending more time waiting in lines to use the ski lifts than they were on the slopes. Lift fees and equipment costs were soaring.

At the same time, there was a growing concern about physical fitness. People were beginning to jog, hike, and go backpacking.

This encouraged Rudy Mattesich and a few friends to form the Ski Touring Council of America in 1962. The purpose of the organization was "to revive the sport of cross-country skiing in America."

A former officer in the Hungarian Army, Mattesich had immigrated to the United States after World War I. Almost from the day he arrived, he began spreading the gospel of cross-country skiing, telling anyone who would listen of the health-giving benefits of the sport, how it enabled a person to escape the crowds, confusions and pressures of modernday life.

EVERYONE CAN SKI

Throughout the 1970s, cross-country skiing grew by leaps and bounds. And it's still growing.

People find it easy to learn. And the risk of injury is low.

Equipment is inexpensive, and you need only enough snow to cover the ground.

You can ski with your friends. It's also one of the few sports that families can enjoy together. In any given year, an estimated 4,000,000 Americans and Canadians go cross-country skiing.

"Anyone can do it where there is snow," says Rudy Mattesich. "Cross-country skiing is an idea whose time has come."

A ski touring family pauses to view the scenery in Inyo National Forest, California.

2 The Equipment You Need

Another of the good things about cross-country skiing is that it requires only a small amount of equipment. And what equipment you do need is not very expensive. A set of golf clubs costs more.

To be equipped for cross-country skiing, you need the following:

Skis	Ski poles
Boots	A lightweight carrying pack
Bindings	

At the beginning, you don't have to buy your skis and other equipment. You can rent what you need at almost all cross-country ski areas. If you're not going to be skiing more than four or five times in a season, it's probably not worthwhile to purchase equipment.

If you do decide to get your own equipment, buy it at a cross-country ski area rather than at a department store or even a sporting goods store. Salespeople at the ski area are better qualified to give you advice.

Have an experienced skier help you to make your purchases. If the ski shop permits it, try out skis, boots, and bindings of different types.

Almost all cross-country ski areas provide equipment on a rental basis.

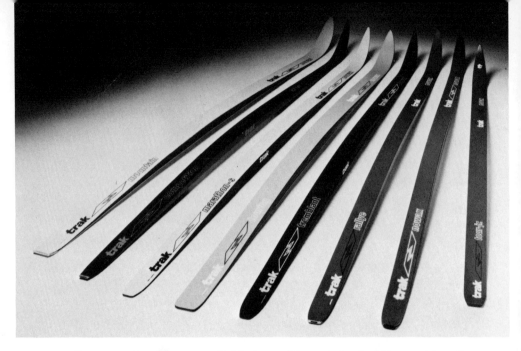

Cross-country skis are available in a wide variety of widths and lengths. Junior touring skis are at extreme right.

Choosing Skis

Your first trip to a ski shop can be a confusing experience. There are dozens of different kinds of cross-country skis from which to choose. They vary in length, width, stiffness, and color.

However, making a decision needn't be difficult, as long as you know the answers to these questions:

How far and how often are you going to be skiing?

Where are you going to be skiing?

Ski Construction

Cross-country skis used to be made of hickory, ash, beech or fir. Nowadays, they're almost always fiberglass.

18

They're not solid fiberglass, but rather a fiberglass sandwich. It has a foam core which is covered by a top and bottom layer of fiberglass. Other layers of harder plastic go over the first two layers. The result is a ski that is much more durable and maneuverable than a ski made of wood.

Camber

The skis you choose must have the right amount of *camber*. To understand camber, imagine a ski placed lengthwise on a shelf or other flat surface at eye level. As you scan the ski from tip to tail, you'll notice an upward curve along the ski bottom. That curve, that arch, is the ski's camber.

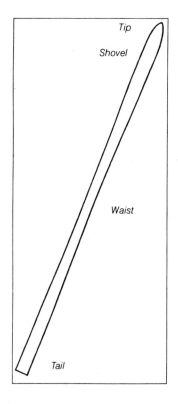

Tip

Shovel

Waist

Tail

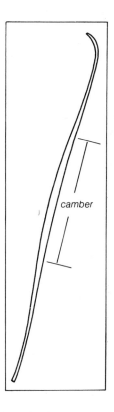

camber

When you put weight on one ski, as in climbing, the camber should flatten out so the middle of the ski makes contact with the snow.

But when you're going downhill and both skis are evenly weighted, the camber at the mid-sections of the skis should ride above the snow. You sail along on the tip and tail sections.

As a beginner, or novice, skier, you want soft-cambered skis, that is, those that have a good amount of flexibility. This is because, as a novice, you haven't developed the strong leg motions of an experienced skier.

The amount of camber your skis should have also depends on your size. The bigger you are, the more camber your skis should have.

Sidecut

Many cross-country skis offer a feature known as *sidecut*. A ski with sidecut is wider at the tip and tail than in the middle. The extra width at these points gives added support and helps in turning.

Whether you choose skis with sidecut or not depends on where you're going to be skiing—across open countryside or at ski areas on prepared tracks.

Track skiing is one of the newest trends in the sport. In track skiing, you ski on a pair of parallel paths cut into the snow. Each is several inches deep and slightly wider than your skis.

Skis with sidecut, because of their extra wideness, cause problems on prepared tracks. The wide parts rub against the sidewalls of the track. As you can imagine, this takes much of the pleasure

When skiing on a prepared track, you need parallel cut skis. ➤

out of touring, slowing you down. The effect is something like trying to run in shoes that are too big for you across a muddy field.

What you need on a prepared track are skis that are the same
width from tip to tail. Skis of this type are known as *parallel cut
skis*. Sidecut skis are best suited for *off-track* skiing.

Types Of Skis

Cross-country skis are divided into four different categories:

- Touring
- Light touring
- Racing
- Mountaineering

Touring Skis

If you, as a beginner, are going to be doing most of your skiing in local parks, over hilly countryside, or through wooded areas, touring skis are your best bet.

Touring skis are closely related to the original cross-country skis. They provide the most surface underfoot, and, thus, the greatest stability. They're heavier than other skis; they're more durable.

Touring skis are the type usually found in rental shops because novice skiers are able to use them without any difficulty. They're also the type often chosen by cross-country veterans who do their skiing in rugged wilderness areas. The extra width of touring skis allows you to tote a heavy backpack, and their strong construction lessens the worry of damage or breakage.

Typical touring skis of the 1980s have soft camber and a good amount of sidecut. Both of these characteristics help in ski control. Soft camber means you can easily flatten the ski, which helps when climbing. Sidecut assures great stability and easier turning.

Light Touring Skis

As you increase in skill and confidence, you may want to

trade in your standard touring skis for light touring skis. Or if you have some experience as a downhill skier, you may want to consider light touring skis from the beginning.

Light touring skis are not only lighter than standard touring skis, they're springier. They respond quickly to the commands of your legs. They absorb bumps and dips with greater efficiency.

While light touring skis have sidecut, it is only a slight amount, usually ranging from 3 mm to 5 mm. One mm (millimeter) is .039 inch, or 39 one-thousandths of an inch. (A typical standard touring ski may have as much as 9 mm of sidecut at the tip, and 5 mm at the tail.) That means that you can use light-weight touring skis on prepared tracks without any difficulty.

Racing Skis

Of the four different types of cross-country skis, racing skis are lightest and most responsive. Made of lightweight, space-age materials, racing skis weigh from two and one-half to three pounds, as compared to an average of about six pounds for standard touring skis.

Racing skis are narrower, too, and most are parallel cut. In recent years, *boat-cut* racing skis have begun to make their appearance. In these, the *waist*, or middle, section is wider than the tips and tails. A boat-cut ski is said to create less drag.

Another characteristic of racing skis is their high cost. Figure on paying about twice as much for a pair of racing skis as you would for standard touring skis.

Mountaineering Skis

For anyone planning to do any wilderness traveling over

rugged terrain, durable, lightweight skis are what are needed. Those are the chief characteristics of *mountaineering* skis.

Their metal edges prevent damage from ice or hard-crusted snow. And they have sidecut so the skier can turn easily when skiing over the untracked countryside.

But they're intended for the specialist, for the expert. For any expedition a beginner might be planning, standard touring skis should serve well.

Waxless Skis

The various types of skis described above are all available as waxless skis. A *waxless ski* has a textured surface along the bottom

Waxless skis have a textured surface that grips the snow when you stride forward.

beneath the boot area. Rub your fingers over it. It feels like a strip of woven fabric.

When you're climbing and stride forward, putting your weight on one ski, the textured surface grips the snow and prevents the ski from slipping back. But when the ski is moving forward, the pattern does not interfere with the ski's ability to glide.

Waxless skis were introduced in the early 1970s. The first waxless skis had a Fishscale® base—a pattern that resembles shingles—molded into the ski bottom.

Waxless skis of the 1980s are available in several different patterns. There are step patterns, bell patterns, and diamond patterns.

Which pattern works best? It depends to some extent on the snow conditions in your area. Waxless skis are best suited for very cold snow, when temperatures are around zero. Others work better when the snow is a bit wet.

Get advice from skiers and ski resort operators in your area. Try to rent two or three different types of waxless skis, and try them out. In other words, experiment before you make your choice.

GETTING THE RIGHT LENGTH

Take the time to be certain that your skis are the right length. Otherwise, problems will result. If your skis are too long, you won't be able to control them properly. They won't always go exactly where you want them to go.

Skis that are too short present other difficulties. They won't *plane* properly, that is, they'll tend to dig in at the tips. You'll constantly be *plowing the snow*, which isn't much fun.

Here's how to be sure you're getting skis of the right length. Stand with your feet flat on the floor and raise one arm straight up in the air. Any pair of skis whose tips touch the wrist of your upraised arm will be the right length for you.

However, there are a couple of exceptions to this rule. If you're particularly light, you will want slightly shorter skis. This is because you have less weight to be distributed on the ski.

On the other hand, if you are heavier than normal for your height, you should pick out a slightly longer ski. You'll then be spreading your weight over a longer surface.

You can also use this chart in selecting skis of the proper length:

Your Height	_Ski Length_
(in inches)	(in centimeters)
4'	150 cm
4'2"	155 cm
4'4"	160 cm
4'6"	165 cm
4'8"	170 cm
4'10"	175 cm
5'	180 cm
5'2"	185 cm
5'4"	190 cm
5'6"	195 cm
5'8"	200 cm
5'10"	205 cm
6'	210 cm

Boots

When you go shopping for ice skates, track shoes, or any

other athletic footwear, you first look for a good fit. That should also be your first thought when buying cross-country ski boots. The pair you decide upon should be comfortable, like a good pair of walking shoes.

There should be one-quarter of an inch of extra space forward of your toes. The rest of the boot should fit snugly. When you flex your foot forward, it should not slide up and down.

Walk around in the boots. They should not feel stiff. When the boot creases, it should not pinch your toes.

Some boots are lined; others, unlined. Lined boots, of course, do a better job of keeping your feet warm when the temperature drops.

Boots are made of a number of different materials, each with its own advantages. Boots of synthetic materials are often water-

Cross-country boots are low-cut, light in weight.

proof. They not only keep water out, but also lock perspiration in, thus causing moisture to build up inside the boot.

Leather boots allow moisture to escape; they "breathe." But leather boots require special care. Never put leather boots in the closet when you return home, and forget about them. And never put them next to a radiator or a stove in an attempt to dry them out.

Instead, stuff the boots with crumpled newspapers and let them dry overnight in a warm room. When the boots are dry, rub them down with a waterproofing compound. Stuff newspapers into the toes so the boots will keep their shape.

Bindings

The *binding* is what fastens your boot to the ski. The cross-country binding is a simple device. Notice the three small pegs that are mounted at the front of the binding soleplate. These pegs, each of which is about the size of a match head, fit into three equally spaced holes in the boot sole.

Once you've fitted the boot sole onto the pegs, a clamp holds it in place. The actual clamping is done with thumb pressure, or, in some cases, by pressing down with the tip of the ski pole.

The binding, incidentally, represents one of the chief differences between cross-country skiing and downhill skiing. The downhill skier is attached to his or her skis in a flat-footed manner, from toe to heel. But the cross-country skier is fastened to the skis only at the toe.

It is an easy step-in, step-out system. More important, it enables you to lift your heel and flex your boot forward on each stride.

The three-peg binding system has changed little over the

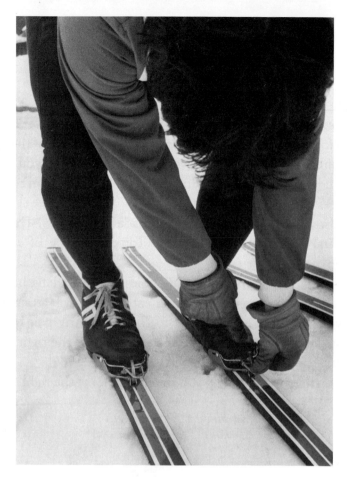

Clamping the boot in place.

years. Newer bindings are made of tough, lightweight metal or rugged plastic. The chief difference between the two materials is weight, with the plastic binding being a bit lighter.

When you try out a pair of bindings, be sure they provide a tight connection between the boots and skis. Check to see that there is no side-to-side boot slip. Unless the boot is held firmly in place by the binding, you won't be able to control the skis properly when turning on downhill runs.

Ski Poles

Poles for cross-country skiing have distinctive tips. They're curved forward. This enables you to pull the poles out of the snow easily after you have skied beyond the point where you thrust them in. Poles for downhill skiing have straight tips. Don't get the two types confused.

Most cross-country ski poles are made of fiberglass. There are also metal poles and tonkin poles. Tonkin, a type of cane or bamboo, can split or crack.

To be sure that you're getting poles of proper length, stand with your feet flat on the floor and extend one arm straight out from your body, so it is parallel to the floor. Any pair of poles that just fits under your outstretched arm will be the right length for you.

This chart will also help you to select poles of the right length:

Your Height	Pole Length
(in inches)	(in centimeters)
4'	90 cm
4'2"	95 cm
4'4"	100 cm
4'6"	105 cm
4'8"	110 cm
4'10"	115 cm
5'	120 cm
5'2"	125 cm
5'4"	130 cm
5'6"	135 cm
5'8"	140 cm
5'10"	145 cm
6'	150 cm

As the chart indicates, poles, like skis, are measured in centi-meters. The difference in height between one pole and the next longer length is five centimeters (about two inches).

If you fall in between pole sizes, get the longer pole. A pole that is a bit longer will not make it harder for you in your efforts to propel yourself over the snow. But a pole that is short for you is of little value.

Check the pole straps. You should be able to adjust the length so that you can wear them with heavy mittens on the coldest days, with light gloves when it's warmer, and also on those occasional afternoons when you can go barehanded.

Look for a pole that has a good-size knob at the top of the handle. The knob enables the pole to fit more securely in the crook of your hand, that is, between the thumb and forefinger. If poles that you own do not have such knobs, you can use several windings of black electrician's tape to create them.

All poles have circular *baskets* mounted about five or six inches above the metal tips. Most baskets are of webbed construction.

Baskets are usually four and one-half to five inches in diameter, which makes them suitable for most snow conditions. But if you're going to be doing most of your skiing in fine, dry powder, you might want to consider baskets of a large diameter to give you a firmer *plant* and greater pushing power.

PACKS

Cross-country skiing would be more fun if you didn't have to wear a *backpack.* You'd move easier; you'd have more freedom.

31

But unless you go skiing for only an hour or so at a time, you'll undoubtedly need a backpack. It's the most convenient method there is of carrying your waxing kit, spare gloves, glasses, an article of clothing you take off, and maybe some snack food.

A waist pack is probably all that you'll need. It straps about your waist with a wide belt and rides just above your fanny. In fact, it's also called a fanny pack. Since it doesn't shift or bounce as you stride, you hardly know it's there.

Waist pack is the easiest, most convenient method of carrying items you may need on the trail.

If your trip is a long one, perhaps taking an entire day, you'll need more supplies and equipment—and a bigger pack—what is called a day pack. It is a rectangular-shaped sack that attaches to your back by means of shoulder straps. There is also a waist strap to hold the pack in place.

A day pack is for more serious carrying.

If you go shopping for a day pack, be sure to select one that's narrow enough to allow your arms to swing back without touching the pack sides. The wider the shoulder straps, the better. The straps should be well padded and adjustable.

You'll see more than a few cross-country skiers wearing what are known as rucksacks. A *rucksack* is a pear-shaped pack that rides fairly high on the back. While it's fine for carrying your books to school, it's not well suited for cross-country ski trips. Since the rucksack doesn't move with your stride, it can become quite a load to carry.

You can use your day pack to carry the various items mentioned earlier in this section, plus a good many others—additional food, drink, extra clothing, a camera, binoculars, and a first-aid kit.

When loading up, put heavy items at the bottom. Lighter weight and frequently used items go toward the top.

EQUIPMENT CARE

Your cross-country equipment will last longer if you take proper care of it.

Skis should be stored in an upright position with the tails down. If you wish, you can strap the skis together at the tails and tips.

Many skiers use masking tape to bind wood skis together, the bottoms facing. Then they insert a small block of wood in between the skis. The block of wood helps to preserve the skis' camber.

Don't stand wet or snow-coated skis on their tails in a warm room. As the snow melts, it can trickle down the skis to form puddles on the floor. It's then possible for the ski tails to soak up some of this water. When you use the skis the next time, the moisture will freeze and the tails crack. Be sure to wipe any snow or moisture from your skis before you store them.

During the summer, store your skis in a cool, dry place. Keep them away from dampness, which can warp them.

Wood skis need special care. Most experts recommend leaving a coating of base wax on the ski bottoms. This helps to prevent the skis from drying out.

Ski Repair

Fiberglass skis are subject to several types of damage. But in most cases you should be able to make the repairs yourself.

You need a small screwdriver, sandpaper, fine steel wool, a small C-shaped clamp, and fast-drying epoxy which is a very strong adhesive. You can buy epoxy in a ski shop or hardware store.

Sometimes the layers that make up a plastic ski start coming apart at the end of the tail or at the tip. To repair the trouble area, apply epoxy to each layer. Press the layers together with your fingers. Then cover the glued portion with cellophane wrap (the kind used to wrap sandwiches), and compress the section with the C-clamp.

Allow the epoxy to dry overnight. The next day, remove the plastic wrap and add a thin coating of epoxy to the outer edge of the trouble area to seal the layers.

Another problem with fiberglass skis involves the small holes into which the screws fit that hold the bindings in place. Through constant untightening and tightening, one or more of the screw holes can become enlarged, and the binding loosens.

To repair an enlarged screw hole, remove the binding. Then fill the hole with epoxy and insert the tip of a golf tee. Press the tee down, then, with a wire cutter, snip it off flush with the surface of the ski.

Next, sand the tee until it is perfectly smooth. Use sandpaper, then fine steel wool. Once the epoxy has hardened, the hole can be redrilled to accept the binding screw.

You can also use epoxy to repair dents or gouges on the top or side surfaces (not the bottoms) of the skis. Be sure the ski is dry before you begin working. Then apply the epoxy to the damaged area, putting on just enough so it will dry flush with the ski surface.

Nicks and gouges on the bottoms of plastic skis can be repaired with the drippings from a special ski candle. You buy these candles at ski shops or sporting goods stores.

Before you begin, remove any dirt or grease from the ski bottoms. The skis should be at room temperature.

Keep a cup of water handy to extinguish the candle in case it starts to burn too fast.

After you light the candle, the first few drops it produces are likely to contain some carbon particles, so let the drops fall into the cup of water.

Hold the candle about one-half inch above the ski and let the drops fall into each gouge. After each gouge is filled with the hot liquid, add one or two more drops. Even though the drippings harden almost instantly, they're still hot. Don't touch them.

After hardening, the excess can be removed with a putty knife. Then use fine steel wool to smooth the plastic.

3 Keeping Warm and Dry

An afternoon of travel over snow-covered farmland or through deep forests can be a memorable experience. But unless you're dressed properly, your memories won't be pleasant ones. The wrong clothing on a cold day can turn your adventure into an uncomfortable, even dangerous ordeal.

The best way to dress for cross-country skiing is to wear several layers of light clothing. This system allows you to adapt what you wear to changes in your body's temperature and the weather.

Not long after you set out on a trail, your body builds up heat. To avoid overheating, you begin shedding clothing, one layer at a time. When you stop for lunch, or toward evening when the temperature begins dropping, you start putting the layers back on again.

If you live in an area of the country where the snow falls, you are likely to already own most of the clothing you will need as a cross-country skier. Whatever you select from your closet, just be certain the garment is cut full or made of a stretch fabric. It has to be able to move as your body moves.

If you're going to be buying most of your skiwear, keep in mind that a great deal of ski clothing is European made, and that European manufacturers use a different sizing scale than American manufacturers. Be sure to try on each garment to be sure you're getting a proper fit.

Proper clothing for cross-country skiing includes warm hat, short jacket, knickers, long socks.

From the skin outward, let's take a look at the cross-country ski outfit, layer-by-layer:

UNDERWEAR

At the bottom, nearest the skin, wear long underwear made of synthetic fibers. Synthetics are recommended because they hold warm air next to your skin and they don't absorb moisture.

On the other hand, wool and cotton soak up perspiration. And if they get wet, they stay wet.

SHIRTS AND PANTS

What you wear over your underwear depends to a great extent on personal preference. Cotton knit shirts are popular. However, if you ski where the weather is colder than average, you may want to wear a wool shirt. Even if it gets very cold, wool will keep you warm.

Be sure the shirt has a long tail. You don't want to be bothered tucking it in during the day.

If you prefer a turtleneck style shirt, choose the type that's fitted with a zipper. In the open position, the collar lies flat, allowing ventilation.

The tradition of wearing knickers for cross-country skiing originated in Europe. The fact that the tradition has survived to this day is easy to understand, because knickers are so practical. They're comfortable. They allow your legs a maximum amount of movement.

When buying knickers, pay especial attention to kneebands, which hold up the socks. They should fit snugly around the upper calf and stretch without losing their shape. Yet they shouldn't be so tight that they cut into your legs. As for the elastic waistband, it should be at least one inch wide.

Bib knickers were recently introduced for cross-country skiing. Worn with a lightweight shirt or sweater, they take the form of a one-piece suit, with the top fitting apronlike over the wearer's head. They thus provide another layer of protection for the upper body.

If you don't plan to wear knickers, simply pick out pants that fit loosely around the knees or are made of stretch fabric. Bib overalls work very well. A boot-top length is available for cross-country skiing.

Never wear tight jeans. They don't permit your body to move freely and do little to keep you warm.

Outerwear

Top off your upper body with a nylon windbreaker. What you shouldn't wear is a heavy insulated parka. It will restrict your arm movement. Poplin and corded cotton are also popular as jacket materials.

When buying a jacket, pay special attention to the zipper. Metal zippers can freeze and jam in cold weather. Look for a zipper made of heavy-duty plastic. And be sure it's equipped with a big pull tab. This enables you to operate the zipper when wearing heavy gloves or mittens.

The jacket pockets should be large enough to carry your

gloves or mittens, glasses, lip balm and other such articles. The pockets should be closed with zippers.

Kangaroo pockets are excellent. A kangaroo pocket fits across the entire front of a pullover jacket. It's a double pocket, in other words.

The jacket's elastic cuffs should be at least one-inch wide. They should fit snugly in order to keep the snow out. But the fit shouldn't be so tight that the cuff squeezes your wrists.

You can also think about a pullover sweater. Choose one that's a mixture of wool and a synthetic fiber. Be sure the sweater is long enough to cover your waistline when you bend over.

Vests are beginning to outdo sweaters in popularity. Made of quilted nylon or one of the other synthetics, vests are lighter in weight than sweaters and less bulky. Of course, their drawback is that they don't protect your arms.

SOCKS

For years, skiers were advised to wear two pairs of socks to keep their feet warm, a light inner pair beneath a heavier outer pair. Not any more. Two pairs of socks cause the feet to perspire, say the experts, and moisture then builds up inside the boots.

Wear one pair of heavy socks. A blend of wool and a synthetic is better than all wool. With wool, snow attaches itself to the socks, and they get damp and sag as a result.

When wearing knickers, be sure to get socks that are long enough to reach over the knee. A gap between the top of the knicker cuff and the top of the sock can ruin a skiing day as surely as a heavy rainfall.

If you're skiing in deep and powdery snow, you'll need a pair of gaiters. Gaiters are like leggings. Made of cloth or leather, they cover the ankle, instep, and sometimes also the lower leg. They prevent deep snow from getting inside your boots.

Most gaiters have elastic stirrups that fit beneath the foot, which keep the gaiters in place. Some have zippers in the front or at the side; others are laced.

Gaiters are also practical because they cover the tops of the ski boots. At the end of the day, the boot laces are dry and soft and easy to untie.

HATS AND CAPS

Always wear some kind of head covering. Much of the body's heat can be lost through an uncovered head. In fact, experiments have shown that a good way to help keep your hands and feet warm is to wear a wool hat that pulls down over the ears.

Hats that are all wool are the best. A wool hat will keep your head warm and dry even if it snows or rains. All you have to do is shake off the moisture from time to time.

Be sure the hat or cap protects your ears, and fits snugly. Nothing can be more frustrating than to have your hat fly off during a downhill run. If you want, you can wear a headband over the ears in addition to the hat.

When picking out a covering for your head, try a *tuque* (rhymes with duke). Believed to be Canadian in origin, the tuque is a loosely-knitted stocking cap with a big tassel on top. It's become a favorite among cross-country skiers.

For skiing in freezing temperatures and when there are high winds, consider the type of knitted headpiece that does double

Don't fail to wear a head covering of some type. Be sure your ears are covered.

duty, covering not only the head, but your face and neck as well. There's an oval opening for the eyes and nose. Should the temperature rise, you roll up the face covering, and it becomes a conventional hat, similar to a sailor's watch cap.

On warmer days, try a peaked baseball cap with a mesh top. The visor will keep the sun out of your eyes. The mesh top allows heat to escape.

43

HANDWEAR

Keeping your hands warm can be a problem. When you're striding along, your body may warm up quickly, but not your hands, since they're not particularly active.

Mitts (the word skiers use for mittens) do a better job of keeping your hands warm than gloves. Mitts can be made of leather or be knitted. Down mitts are gaining in popularity.

Gloves are preferred by many skiers because they enable you to get a firmer grip on the ski poles. One type of glove has a leather palm, a cloth back, and light insulating material inside. Wool knit gloves with leather palms are also worn frequently.

Some skiers get both warmth and good gripping power by

Gloves or mitts? Gloves enable you to grip your ski poles better but mitts are warmer.

wearing two pairs of gloves. The inner pair is thin, usually a cotton and rayon blend. The outer glove is a wool and synthetic-fiber blend, again with a leather palm to cut down on wear.

EYE PROTECTION

Snow reflects an enormous amount of the sun's light, so much of it, in fact, that it can irritate and cause discomfort to your eyes. On all except the dullest days, you're likely to need protection from the glare.

You can wear either glasses or goggles. If you wear glasses, be sure to pick lenses of good size. Glasses with small lenses can allow glare to seep in around the edges. Be sure the lenses are shatterproof.

As for the tint, choose gray, green, or a combination of both. On overcast days, wear yellow lenses. Avoid lenses that are tinted pink or blue.

Special plastic goggles are available for skiing. Goggles fit more securely than glasses. Be sure the lens has a flat surface like a pane of window glass, not curved. Otherwise, your vision will be distorted.

One problem with goggles is that they tend to fog up, and you have to stop and wipe the lens. This is probably the chief reason more skiers wear glasses than goggles.

Throughout the day, you want your clothing to keep you comfortably warm. You shouldn't ever feel chilled. On the other hand, you should avoid sweating. At the first sign of either of these, adjust your clothing layers immediately.

4 Before You Start Out

Even if you're only a beginner at cross-country skiing, you'll still be able to travel about twice as fast on skis as you do when you walk. But, skiing makes greater physical demands upon your body. Unless you're in good condition, you won't be able to enjoy cross-country skiing to the fullest.

There are many ways to get into shape. Bicycling is excellent. It not only develops the leg muscles, but the heart and lungs as well. Jumping rope is recommended, too. And you can do it indoors, which can't be said of bicycling.

Jogging, swimming, tennis, and soccer are other sports that can help to prepare you for cross-country skiing. Taking part in one of these sports about three times a week will help you get physically fit.

MUSCLE-BUILDING EXERCISES

If you're like most beginner skiers, you'll find that your arms tire more quickly than your legs.

A good exercise to strengthen your arm muscles is called the chair lift. Stand in back of an ordinary straight-back wooden chair and, squatting down, reach out and grasp the chair seat at the sides. As you straighten your legs and stand up, lift the chair seat as high as the level of your head.

Repeat the exercise three or four times. Work up to ten repetitions, or even more.

You can also work to strengthen your legs. One easy exercise is to stand erect, your feet about shoulder width apart. Then thrust your hands forward and bend your knees until you've assumed a half-squat position. Return to the starting position and do it again.

Be sure to do the exercise slowly. You should be able to do eight to ten repetitions, but keep trying to increase the number.

Here's another leg-strengthening exercise you can try: With your back up against the wall, pretend you are sitting in a straight-back chair. Your thighs should be parallel to the floor.

Press away from the wall with your lower back, putting pressure on your legs and feet. Notice how the muscles of your thighs quickly tire. Try to hold the position for 15 seconds.

Relax; stand erect; try it again.

The stride you use as a cross-country skier should be relaxed and rhythmic. Here's an exercise meant to help you develop that rhythm: Stand with your weight evenly distributed on the balls of your feet, then start jumping up and down, flexing your knees on each bounce. It's the same movement you use when skipping rope.

Now, as you continue to jump, get your arms going. As you swing your right arm forward, swing your left arm back. Time the movement of your arms with your knee bends.

Do the exercise slowly at first, then start speeding up.

Waxing Your Skis

Waxing is one of the basic skills of cross-country skiing. It's as important to your enjoyment of the sport as knowing how to stride and glide.

All cross-country skis need waxing. Even waxless skis perform better when a coat of wax is applied to the tip and tail areas.

When your skis are properly waxed, you can glide with ease over level terrain or when going downhill. But at the same time, you're able to climb hills of modest size without sliding backward. In other words, wax enables your skis to both glide and grip.

Waxing would be a simple matter if it were not for the different types of snow you encounter during the average skiing season. Snow can be light and fluffy; it can be heavy and wet. Since these differences affect how your skis perform, wax has to be chosen and applied so as to match snow conditions.

For dry and powdery snow, you need a hard wax. For wet snow, you need a soft wax.

As this suggests, the first thing you must do is judge the character of the snow. Check the thermometer. If the temperature at ground level is well below freezing (below 25°F or −4°C), the snow is likely to be dry. If the temperature is well above freezing (above 35°F or 2°C), the snow is undoubtedly wet.

Sometimes, however, temperature readings from outdoor thermometers can be misleading. If the thermometer happens to be exposed to bright sun, the reading can deceive you. The same is true if the thermometer happens to be in a shaded, windswept spot.

A better method of checking the character of the snow is to squeeze a handful in your gloved hand. Watch what happens

Called a waxometer, this thermometer gives waxing advice.

when you open your hand. If the snow is loose and dry and blows away, it's dry. If it clumps up and forms a snowball, it's wet.

How to Wax

Whenever possible, wax your skis indoors. It's much easier. Many cross-country ski areas have heated waxing huts for this purpose.

You must begin with clean, dry skis. Wax won't stick to wet or dirty surfaces.

If your skis have been carried for a long distance while clamped in a cartop carrier, they may be coated with a film of road dirt. You'll have to scour them before they can be waxed.

For this reason, it's a good idea to cover the skis with plastic wrapping before putting them in a cartop carrier. This protects them from road grime.

Begin by giving the skis a good wax base, applying several coats of hard wax with short, rapid strokes. Rub in each coat with a cork.

The colder and more powdery the snow, the smoother the wax should be. You do not need to wax the tracking groove that runs down the middle of the ski bottoms.

Waxes for warmer conditions, above freezing, should be applied on top of the base coat. If the weather keeps getting warmer during the day, it may be necessary to apply wax several times or you may have to change to a different type of wax.

If conditions begin to turn slushy, you'll probably have to use a *klister* wax. Klister waxes are very sticky and difficult to apply. It takes as much as a quarter of an hour for some types of klister to dry.

Test your waxing job by skiing. Try skiing uphill. If you slip, you may have applied the wrong kind of wax. Or you haven't applied enough wax. Simply adding more wax may solve the problem.

Also try skiing downhill. If you have to push with your poles to overcome stickiness, then your skis have too much grip.

First, check whether you've used the right type of wax. It may be too soft. Second, check to see whether you've applied too much wax. If that seems to be the case, scrape some off. Begin at the tail and work toward the binding. Smooth the remaining wax with a cork.

There are a great many different kinds of waxes available.

Applying the base coat is easy.

Old wax has to be scraped off before new can be applied.

Some are packaged in small foil-wrapped cylinders, about the size of flashlight batteries. Others are shaped in big blocks, each about the size of a pound of butter. Waxes also come in tubes, like toothpaste, and in spray cans, like paint. Even expert skiers get bewildered by the assortment.

To avoid confusion, use the waxes of only one manufacturer. Follow the direction on the package labels.

And keep in mind these general rules:

- Use hard wax for dry snow.
- Use soft wax for wet snow.

Waxing Waxless Skis

You don't have to wax waxless skis for grip. In fact, if you did apply wax to the textured area, you could ruin the ski's ability to grip.

But you can wax waxless skis for protection against moisture and so they will glide better. You only wax the tip and tail sections. Apply a base wax from the tip of the ski to the beginning of the textured area. Also wax from the tail to the point where the textured surface ends.

Check the tip and tail sections during the season. The wax may wear away, in which case you should wax again.

THE WIND-CHILL FACTOR

What's the temperature? That's the question every skier asks before setting out.

But what the thermometer happens to be reading is only part of the story. Wind speed is the other part. The greater the wind's velocity, the colder it really is.

The National Weather Service has devised a mathematical formula to express the relationship between temperature and the wind's speed. It is called the *wind-chill* formula. Meteorologists used the formula to develop the chart on page 54.

To use the chart, you have to know both the temperature and the speed of the wind. Suppose the thermometer reads 25°F and the wind's velocity is 10 miles per hour (mph).

According to the chart, the equivalent chill temperature is 9°F. In other words, you should dress as if the thermometer was reading 9°F, not 25°F.

Wind-Chill Factor Table

Temperature (degrees Fahrenheit)

| 35 | 30 | 25 | 20 | 15 | 10 | 5 | 0 | − 5 | −10 | −15 | −20 |

Equivalent Chill Temperature

Wind speed (mph)	35	30	25	20	15	10	5	0	− 5	−10	−15	−20
Calm	35	30	25	20	15	10	5	0	− 5	−10	−15	−20
5	33	27	21	16	12	7	1	− 6	−11	−15	−20	−26
10	21	16	9	2	− 2	− 9	−15	−22	−27	−31	−38	−45
15	16	11	1	− 6	−11	−18	−25	−33	−40	−45	−51	−60
20	12	3	− 4	− 9	−17	−24	−32	−40	−46	−52	−60	−68
25	7	0	− 7	−15	−22	−29	−37	−45	−52	−58	−67	−75
30	5	− 2	−11	−18	−26	−33	−41	−49	−56	−63	−70	−78
35	3	− 4	−13	−20	−27	−35	−43	−53	−60	−67	−72	−83
40	1	− 4	−15	−22	−29	−36	−45	−54	−62	−69	−76	−87

You should learn to read certain of nature's signs as an indication of the wind's velocity. When chimney smoke rises straight up and the branches of bare trees are motionless, then the wind is calm.

But when the branches of trees sway, open water is being rippled, and you can feel the wind's coldness on your skin, the velocity of the wind is approaching 12 mph.

It's more serious when the wind whistles through tree branches and powdery snow gets blown about and piled into drifts. These are indications that the wind velocity is between 12 and 25 mph.

When whole trees bend, snow drifts into enormous piles, and walking into the wind takes special effort, the wind's speed is in excess of 25 mph.

Before you leave home, determine the wind's speed, and plan

accordingly. If it's a calm day, and the wind is not a factor, you can head out into open country. But if it's blustery, you'll be better off planning a route that takes you through sheltered country.

Also figure out the wind-chill factor before you depart. It makes no sense to plan for a day of 25°F when it's *really* 9°F.

FROSTBITE

Too much exposure to severe cold can cause frostbite, a condition in which body tissue becomes injured or even damaged by freezing. You should learn to recognize the symptoms of frostbite and know what to do should they occur.

Frostbite is easy to prevent. The feet and fingers usually fall victim to frostbite first, so don't let them get cold in the first place. Follow the advice set down in the previous chapter concerning your selection of warm socks and mitts.

If your fingers should begin to get cold, even though you're wearing mitts or gloves, swing your arms vigorously in full circles. This should increase your circulation, warming your fingers all the way to the tips.

Cold toes are more of a problem. Try striding faster.

If this doesn't seem to do much good, it may be that your boot laces are too tight. Stop, unclamp your boots from the skis, loosen the laces, and stamp your feet. Try to restore circulation to your toes.

If this doesn't work, it might be best to stop and build a small fire. Use the fire's heat to warm your feet gradually. Rub them gently as you're warming them. Once your feet are warm, get moving again as quickly as possible and keep up a brisk pace for as long as you can.

Despite such efforts, frostbite can still occur. If any part of your skin turns pale and glassy, assume that frostbite is beginning to develop.

Treat the stricken area by covering it or gently warming it. Don't rub frostbitten tissue. You can break the skin.

Never apply snow or cold water to a frostbitten area. In the past, skiers were often incorrectly advised to do so.

Never encourage someone with frostbitten toes or fingers to continue skiing. Serious injury can result. The person should be carried.

If you can get him or her indoors, by all means do so. But do not get the injured frostbitten area near a radiator or hot stove. Do not apply a hot water bottle or use a heat lamp. Too much heat can do more harm than good.

HYPOTHERMIA

When traveling long distances on skis, you use large amounts of the body's heat. In most cases, no harm is done. To compensate for the heat loss, you simply add another layer of clothing or start moving faster, or both.

But the body can lose more heat than it has produced. If the heat loss continues until the body temperature drops below normal, a condition known as *hypothermia* results. Hypothermia can cause death if it goes unrecognized and untreated.

Most people associate hypothermia with sub-zero temperatures, but the truth is that the condition occurs with greater frequency when it is only mildly cold, with the air temperature between 20°F and 30°F (−6°C to −1°C). Skiers don't look at these temperatures as being dangerous, and they get careless as a result.

It is much easier to spot the beginning of hypothermia in others than in oneself—another reason why you should never set out on a trail alone. The first symptoms are usually shivering and excessive fatigue. The skin becomes pale, speech is slurred, and the skier is likely to start stumbling or lurching.

Whenever the day is cold, and there's rain or wet snow, and a biting cold wind blows without letup, every skier in your party should keep an eye on the others for signs, or symptoms, of hypothermia. A person exhibiting the first signs may not believe that he or she is a potential victim. But begin to treat the person anyway. Ignore the symptoms, and you may be placing a life in jeopardy.

In treating a hypothermia victim, the first step is to make him or her warmer. Give the person more clothing, a windbreaker, a jacket, or wool sweater.

Make the victim drink a warm, nonalcoholic beverage. Cocoa is highly recommended for its energy producing benefits.

If the person's clothes are wet, bring him or her indoors as quickly as possible. Strip off the wet clothes and get the person into dry ones. Give him or her warm drinks.

Like many problems of this type, hypothermia can be prevented by taking certain precautions. Wear clothing to suit the conditions you're going to encounter. If whatever clothing you're wearing fails to keep you warm and dry, put an end to your outing. If you get wet on a cold day, look for shelter as quickly as you can.

If you're skiing vigorously and sweating, be sure to drink water or other fluids at regular intervals. Stop for snacks.

Take at least one short rest every hour. Watch the other members of your party for signs of fatigue.

Hypothermia is a serious matter. But if you're sensible and think ahead, you need never reach a stage that even borders on hypothermia.

Frequent stops to rest are important.

5 The Basic Skills

You'll often hear it said that if a person can walk, he or she can ski. The statement isn't completely true, but it makes the point: Cross-country skiing is easy.

Even though the sport is not difficult to learn, it's a good idea to get some instruction at first. Almost all cross-country ski areas offer group lessons. They're usually free or cost very little. You join a handful of other beginners in a class that lasts less than an hour.

Cross-country ski lessons are also being offered at YMCAs and high schools, at ski shops and sporting goods stores. Inquire at such places in your neighborhood.

If you don't take any lessons, at least watch a skilled skier stride and glide before you actually put on skis and try moving around yourself. It can be an instructor at a local ski area or perhaps someone who races on skis.

Study the person carefully. Try to pick out the basic movements that enable him or her to move fast and be nimble.

However, keep in mind that you will not ski exactly like the instructor, the racer, or any of your friends. No two individuals

Skiing lessons will help you to develop the right technique.

Young skiers follow their instructor through the village of Jackson, New Hampshire.

ski alike. Just as in walking, everyone has a different style, a different gait. What you have to do is develop your own efficient way of moving on skis, your own style, following the fundamentals set down in this chapter.

First Time On Skis

The first time you try out skis, pick out level ground. You can use your backyard, as long as it is snow covered. You can use a football field, a baseball diamond, or the fairway of a golf course.

All you really need is a few inches of snow over a soft base. Avoid concrete, asphalt, or other paved surfaces. They can damage the bottoms of your skis.

Once you've put on your skis, take a pole in each hand. Use them to help you keep your balance.

When you grip the pole, thrust your hand through the loop of the strap from underneath. When your fingers encircle the handle, the strap should be sandwiched between the pole and the point where your thumb and index finger join. This method of gripping gives you better control over the poles.

If you've never been on skis before, they're going to feel awkward to you. But a few simple exercises will help you to get accustomed to them.

Notice how you can lift each heel, but the toes remain clamped in place. It's because the heels are free to move up and down that you can move fast and efficiently on your skis.

Now, try this exercise: Concentrate your weight on your right ski, and slide the left ski forward. Slide it as far forward as

Your hand should go through the strap from underneath.

You can lift each heel, but toes stay clamped in place.

you can. Notice how your right knee bends and your right heel lifts from the ski.

Switch feet. Slide the right ski forward, and notice how the left heel lifts from the ski.

Keep repeating this drill, first sliding one ski forward, then the other.

Now try moving forward over open ground. Pick out an object about 100 feet away—a tree, bush, or rock—and head for it.

Start with your weight on your left ski and slide the right ski forward a couple of feet. Shift your weight to the right ski and slide the left ski forward.

You don't have to lift the skis from the ground. Just keep sliding along until you've reached your goal. Then go back to the starting point.

Try for rhythmic strides. Lean forward slightly as you go. Be sure your heels are moving freely with each stride.

When your right leg goes forward, your left arm should go forward. The left leg and right arm also move forward together.

Don't look down at your feet. Keep your eyes on the trail, looking at least one ski length ahead.

THE KICK

So far you've just been getting accustomed to your skis. If a ski instructor were to see you moving along by sliding from one ski to the other, he or she would be certain to frown and call out to you, "You're just shuffling. You're not skiing. You have to develop a kick."

A *kick* in skiing is nothing like a soccer kick or a football kick.

It's a motion in which you push off from the ball of one foot, moving forward on the other ski. Unless you develop a good kick, you'll never be able to enjoy cross-country skiing.

To understand the kick movement, imagine you're skateboarding. Your left foot is on the board. Your right foot is doing the pushing. It's the push-and-glide motion that is the basis of skiing's kick.

Try using one ski in skateboard fashion. Bring your feet together, putting the right ski a few inches ahead of the left. Push

It's like skating—you push from one ski, glide on the other.

off from the left ski, glide on the right.

When you have the "feel" of pushing from the left ski and gliding on the right, try it on the opposite side. Push off from the right ski, gliding on the left. When you begin to slow down, push from the right ski again.

Now, keep repeating the exercise, but alternate sides.

As you finish pushing off from one ski, you shift your weight, glide, and push off from the other ski. Be sure to lift each ski as you bring it forward.

Push from the right ski, glide on the left.

Push from the left, glide on the right. It's much like ice skating or roller skating.

At first you're not likely to make much forward progress, perhaps only a foot or so. Relax—loosen your hips—stretch out. Little by little, your kick will get better.

Using Your Poles

Once you understand the basics of the cross-country stride and are able to make good speed, you can begin using your poles. Proper use of the poles gives you added power.

Suppose you're striding along a trail. As you swing the left ski forward, you thrust your right arm forward. You plant the right ski pole at the same time you start the right ski forward.

If your timing is right, the basket of the right ski pole should go into the snow at a point even with the left foot. This is the diagonal system of poling. As one ski goes forward, so does the pole on the opposite side.

If you were able to watch a skier from above, you'd see that

As one ski goes forward, so does the pole on the opposite side.

his arms formed one diagonal line, the legs another, and the two lines crisscrossed.

Keep a firm grip on the poles, but not a tight one. If you clench the pole handles tightly, you'll create tension in your wrists and forearms, and you won't be able to swing your arms naturally.

If you're having problems poling, try skiing for a few hundred feet without using any poles. Exaggerate the swing of your arms as you stride. When you're swinging your arms freely and fully on both sides, start using the poles again.

66

Double Poling

Sometimes it will be to your advantage to use a double-pole technique. You double-pole almost any time you go from flat terrain to a downhill or uphill slope. In such cases, it's the more efficient way of getting up speed.

To double pole, you bring both poles forward at the same time, plant them, and push off from both simultaneously.

Double poling can help you when you start going uphill or downhill.

After you push off, both arms should be extended behind you, the poles almost parallel to the ground.

Practice double poling at the top of a gentle slope. Stride ahead on one ski, planting both poles and pushing off.

How To Fall And Get Up

If you're a skiing beginner, you can be sure you're going to take a few spills. But since the snow is there to cushion your landing, falling is seldom a serious matter.

In cross-country skiing, falling is seldom a serious matter.

68

If you should start falling during a downhill run, try to make it as gentle a fall as you can. Squat down low and either sit down or topple over to one side. Or steer into a soft snowbank.

If you fall in deep and powdery snow, it may be difficult for you to get back up onto your skis. The first thing to do is to bring both of your skis underneath your body, and then slowly stand up. Use your poles for support.

Getting up is a greater problem when you're partly buried in the snow after a fall. You'll probably have to remove your skis in order to get free. To get the skis back on, try this: place the skis flat on the snow, one on each side of you. Then, using your arms, raise your feet to snow level and onto the skis. Using your poles for support, stand up.

Advanced Skills

Turning and stopping. Going uphill, going downhill. These are skills you have to have to be a polished skier. If you can move around on your skis with confidence, they shouldn't be difficult for you to learn.

How To Go Uphill

The cross-country method of ascending, or going up, a slope is to ski straight up it, almost as if the hill were a level stretch of ground. If your skis are properly waxed, you should be able to stride and glide uphill without great difficulty.

Practice uphill skiing on a gentle slope at first. Concentrate on getting each ski to grip the snow firmly. Press down hard.

Shortening your strides and leaning forward more from the waist will help you to get more gripping power. Increase your knee bend, too.

Of course, you're not going to get much glide when you're heading uphill. And if it's a steep slope, you may not get any glide at all.

When the slope is a gentle one, you should be able to ski straight up it.

When the slope becomes so steep that your skis start sliding back, try steering slightly to the right or left so that you're ascending the hill diagonally. Exaggerate the forward lean of your body.

The Sidestep

Some hills may be so steep that there's no chance you will be able to ski up them, even if you try proceeding diagonally. You then use one of two other methods of ascent—the sidestep or the herringbone.

The *sidestep* is the easiest of the two. It's exactly the same as walking up a staircase sideways, one step at a time.

It sounds simple, and it is. To sidestep up a slope, first turn your skis 90 degrees to either the right or left so that they lie across the slope. Lift the uphill ski and step sideways up the hill with it. Then pick up the downhill ski and plant it alongside the uphill one.

Keep edging your way up the hill in that fashion—first moving the uphill ski sideways, then bringing the downhill ski alongside it. The steeper the slope, the shorter your steps will be.

The Herringbone

If you're faced with a long, steep slope, sidestepping your way up will take a good deal of time. The *herringbone* is a more efficient

Using the herringbone, young skiers ascend a slope at Quebec's Mont Sainte Anne Park.

method of going up. But it's also the more difficult. In addition, it can tire you quickly if you're not in top-flight condition.

The herringbone gets its name from the pattern the skis etch in the snow as you climb. It looks like a fishbone (not necessarily that of a herring, *any* fishbone).

Herringbone leaves fishbone pattern in the snow.

Try the herringbone on a gentle slope first. Spread the tips of your skis wide apart, with the tails together, so that a "V" is formed. In order to ascend, step first with one ski and then the other, always keeping the angle of the "V".

Use your poles to keep from slipping. As your left ski goes forward, plant the right pole and push from it.

The problem that beginners have with the herringbone is that the tail of the striding ski sometimes is planted so that it crisscrosses the tip of the ski that's flat to the snow. This gives you the same feeling you might get if someone tied your shoelaces together. To avoid crossing your skis, be sure to make each stride as long as possible, so that the tail of the striding ski goes beyond the tip of the other ski.

Going Downhill

Cross-country skis, being light in weight and highly maneuverable, provide exciting fun on a downhill run.

Begin by practicing on low hills that flatten gradually at the bottom so you can glide to a slow stop. As your confidence and skill develop, move to steeper slopes.

Keep your skis comfortably apart and simply coast. Bend forward from your ankles. Bend your knees, too. When you flex your knees and ankles, your legs act as shock absorbers, cushioning any bumps you might encounter.

Although you bend forward, your weight should be concentrated more toward your heels than your toes. Of course, this means that your heels will always be flat to the skis.

Going downhill, keep your skis apart and just coast.

If your position is correct, you won't be able to see your boots when you look down. They'll be blocked by your knees.

If you have trouble keeping your balance, squat down low, really low, as you begin your descent. Don't use your poles. You should be able to reach down and touch the snow on either side. This position lowers your center of gravity, and you're much less likely to lose your balance.

When you are able to go all the way down the slope in a squat position without falling, move to a position halfway between squatting and standing. Next, try standing, being sure to bend from the waist and at the knees.

When you begin using your poles on downhill runs, hold them with the tips pointed back. What you must not do is hold the tips in front of you, your idea being to jab them into the ground to slow your speed or prevent a fall. There are simpler and safer methods to slow down and stop, and they're explained later in this chapter.

Always grasp the poles by only the handles on a downhill run. Don't put your hands through the straps. Should the basket of a pole get snagged in the brush, you want to be able to release the pole immediately. If you're unable to do so, you can wrench a wrist.

Once you become skilled in downhill skiing, try shifting your weight, first to one side, then to the other, as you make your descent. Do it slowly, rhythmically. This serves as an introduction to the stopping and turning maneuvers you're going to learn.

How To Stop

Young skiers know how to stop from the very first time they put on skis. They simply squat low, then sit back on their skis and let their hands drag at their sides.

While the sit-back stop is simple and works, expert skiers prefer another method. It's called the *snowplow* stop. The name comes from the fact that your skis are made to plow the snow in slowing you down.

The Snowplow Stop

Imagine you're whisking down a slope. Your knees and ankles are flexed. Your weight is back on your heels.

To slow down, force the tails of your skis outward until they form a "V" and begin plowing the snow. The farther apart you spread the tails, the greater the braking effect. You can also make

The snowplow stop. By plowing the snow, skis brake your forward motion.

the maneuver work better by bending your knees more, in a knock-kneed position.

Keep your weight evenly distributed on both skis. Should you put more weight on the left ski, say, you'll find yourself veering to the right.

Some beginning skiers have difficulty with the snowplow stop because when they thrust out the tails, the tips meet or cross, resulting in a loss of control. This is usually caused by lack of experience. You simply aren't aware of where the tips are going to go when you thrust the tails outward.

If you have this problem, practice the snowplow on flat terrain from a standing-still position. Press the tails outward, keeping aware of the tips. Then bring the skis parallel again. Repeat two or three times, or until you have a sense of how the tips behave.

How To Turn

There are several ways a cross-country skier can turn. The method you should use depends on your skill and experience.

The Step Turn

The simplest turn, made from a standing-still position, is the step turn, or, to use its more descriptive name, the step-around turn. It's a cinch. Keeping the tail of the ski to the ground, you raise the tip and move the ski sideways. Then raise the tip of the other ski and bring it alongside the first. Keep repeating the maneuver until you're facing in the desired direction.

As the skis are moved, they make marks in the snow that resemble the spokes of a wheel. In fact, the step turn is sometimes called the *wagon wheel*.

You don't necessarily have to be on level terrain to do a step turn. You can also use it on a slope, even a fairly steep slope, but you have to get your ski poles into the act. Position your skis so they lie across the hill. Then plant your poles on the downhill side of the skis, and lean on them as you sidestep your way through the turn.

The Snowplow Turn

The snowplow turn is done during a downhill run. If you can execute a snowplow stop without any difficulty, the snowplow turn shouldn't be any problem for you.

Try turning on a gentle slope first. As you ski down, ease your skis into a snowplow position. Start shifting your weight back and forth from one ski to the other. Notice how you start tracing a zigzag route down the hill.

Now shift your weight to one ski, and keep it there. If it's the left ski you've weighted, you will turn to the right. When you've turned as far as you can without slowing down too much, weight the other ski and change direction.

If you only turn part of the way, it's likely to be because you haven't kept your weight concentrated over the *outside* ski. You must lean the upper part of your body over that ski, and hold that position to keep the turn going.

The Skating Turn

The *skating turn* is an advanced turn that enables you to change direction with little loss of speed. Practice the skating turn on level terrain at first.

Suppose you want to turn to the right. Concentrate your weight on the left ski. Pick up the right ski and place it in the direction of the turn.

When you put the right ski down, spring on to it. Then complete the turn by bringing the left ski parallel to the right.

In the skating turn, you spring from one ski to the other as you make a change in direction.

7 Skiing Fun

Like bicycling or motoring, cross-country skiing demands that you obey certain rules of the road. They help to make your outing safe and enjoyable.

The first rule of safe skiing is to pick out a trail that matches your ability. A trail for beginners is likely to loop through the woods for a distance of two or three kilometers (1.2 to 1.8 miles). An intermediate trail runs from five to ten kilometers (3.1 to 6.2 miles), while a trail for experienced skiers can range from twenty to thirty kilometers (12.4 to 18.6 miles) and up.

A standard trail marking system also points out which trails are easy and which are difficult. Look for the trail marking signs. They also indicate trail conditions and hazards.

No matter what type of trail you select, plan your day carefully. Be prepared for the unexpected—a piece of equipment can break; an accident can occur.

But most difficulties can be avoided if you follow these simple rules of the road.

Before you start out, examine your skis and poles, checking

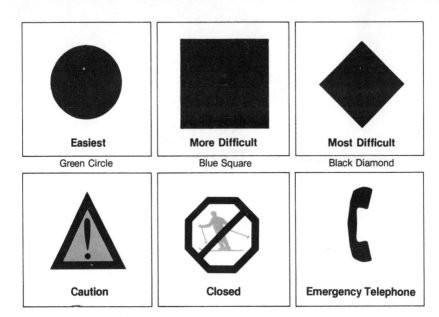

Easiest	More Difficult	Most Difficult
Green Circle	Blue Square	Black Diamond
Caution	Closed	Emergency Telephone

Standard trail markings.

SKIER RESPONSIBILITIES

There are elements of risk in skiing that common sense and personal awareness can help reduce.

1. Maintain control of your speed and direction at all times.

2. Ski in a manner that does not endanger others.

3. Do not stop where you obstruct a trail or are not visible by others.

4. Obey all signs and posted warnings.

5. Keep off closed trails.

6. Report all accidents.

BE SAFETY CONSCIOUS!

for cracks and other imperfections. Inspect the screws that fasten the bindings to the skis. Tighten the screws if they need it. Check the pins that connect the baskets to the poles. If you should lose a basket in deep snow while you are out on a trail, the pole becomes useless.

• If you're renting equipment, be sure your boots fit properly and the bindings clamp the boots to the skis securely.

• Gather all the information you can about the route you're taking. Obtain a trail map at the lodge or rental hut. Check weather reports and trail conditions. Find out what waxes are being recommended.

• Once out on the trail, keep a reasonable distance from other skiers. When starting uphill, watch out for skiers coming down. They are moving faster, so give them the right of way, even if it means you have to get off the track.

• If the trail is made up of more than one track, always keep to the right. Groups of skiers should always ski in single file.

• You can pass a slower skier at any time, using any free track, or, if necessary going outside the tracks. Always allow a faster skier to pass. However, you don't have to get out of the track to permit the overtaking skier to go by.

• If you stop on a busy trail, leave the track.

• If you should come upon an injured skier, give assistance. One member of your party should stay with him or her, while two others go for help.

• In case of an emergency, contact the *National Ski Patrol* representative at the ski area. He or she is trained in handling injuries and assisting in cold weather emergencies.

Cross-country skiers always proceed in single file.

• If you picnic, don't litter. Everything you carry in should be carried out.

• Check local rules and regulations before you build a fire. Keep in mind that snow and freezing temperatures do not prevent forest fires.

OFF-TRAIL TRAVEL

As you become experienced in cross-country skiing, you may want to leave established skiing areas and head out into unfamiliar country. Off-trail travel provides the greatest thrills that cross-country skiing has to offer. But it also increases the risk.

You should always be in the company of others when you take part in such a venture. Your party should consist of at least four experienced skiers. Be sure they have the strength to take part in what might become a difficult trek.

Planning Your Trip

If you don't prepare and plan, getting lost is always a possibility. Falling snow can hide familiar landmarks. Gathering darkness can change the way the countryside looks.

Never set out into unfamiliar country without a reliable compass and a detailed map. The best maps are the U.S. Geological Survey topographical maps. They are prepared in wonderful detail, showing hills and valleys, roads and railroads, and cities and towns.

To obtain a map covering the area in which you're located, first get an index map for your state. From the index map, you'll be able to order the map-section you want. Map indexes are free. The maps themselves range in price from $1.75 to $3.

Requests for indexes covering the states east of the Mississippi River, including Minnesota, should be sent to the Branch of Distribution, U.S. Geological Survey, 1200 South Eads St., Arlington, VA 22202.

Requests for indexes for the states west of the Mississippi River, including Louisiana, should be sent to the Branch of Distribution, U.S. Geological Survey, P.O. Box 25286, Federal Center, Denver, CO 80225.

Indexes and maps prepared by the U.S. Geological Survey

are also available from many hundreds of private map dealers. They are listed in the Yellow Pages of your telephone directory under MAPS.

Canadian maps that are similar to U.S. Geological Survey maps are available from the Canada Map Office, Department of Energy, Mines and Resources, 615 Booth St., Ottawa, Ontario KIA 0E9. If you're interested in the province of Ontario, or any of the provinces east of Ontario, ask for Index No. 1. The provinces west of Ontario are covered in Index No. 2.

For maps of national forests, contact the U.S. Forest Service, Department of Agriculture, Washington, DC 20250. For the national parks, write the National Park Service, Department of the Interior, Washington, DC 20240.

Use your map to lay out your route. Decide on your destination, perhaps a hilltop, a wildlife area, a lodge, or a ranger station.

Study the map carefully to become familiar with the countryside that you'll be covering. Learn the main features, such as roads, wooded areas, hills, lakes, streams, marshes and swamps. You want to keep surprises to a minimum.

Measure the distance you plan to cover. Your first treks should be short ones. At no point along the route should you be any more than half a mile from a highway or occupied lodge or residence.

If you're in remote country and are uncertain about exactly where you are, stop, sit down, take out your map, and study it. Look for landmarks that will help you to establish exactly where you are. Then decide on a route that will get you back to familiar territory. Check the map frequently to be sure you're on the right course.

If you plan your trip wisely, not embarking on a venture that

Never venture into unfamiliar territory without a detailed map.

is beyond what you can do, it's difficult to get lost. After all, you can always reverse your route and follow your ski tracks back.

What To Take

You should always pack along emergency equipment and supplies when you leave established trails. Lightweight survival kits are prepared by several firms and sold at camping supply stores.

Of course, you can make up your own kit. Among the essential items it should contain are such high-calorie food snacks as chocolate, honey or maple syrup, dried fruits, and nuts, including peanuts, pecans, almonds, and cashews.

Your kit should contain matches and a fire starter. First-aid supplies are also vital.

Breaking a ski tip when you're in a remote area can be a disaster. Many ski shops sell slip-on emergency tips, made of plastic. Don't fail to set out with a spare tip.

A pocket knife and a length of nylon rope can come in handy. A few feet of masking tape can be useful in making emergency repairs.

If you get lost, a whistle can be used to attract the attention of

Pack along emergency supplies.

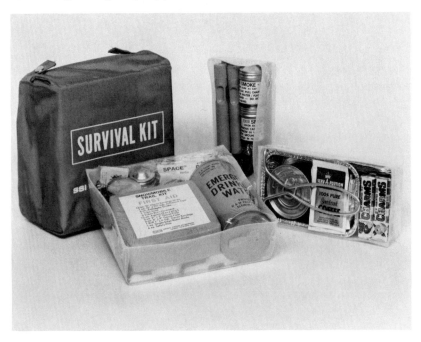

a rescue party. Signal flares or small smoke grenades have the same use.

Rules of the Road

Here are other rules of safety and etiquette you should follow anytime you leave established trails:

• Before you and your party set out, be sure to advise others of your exact plans. For instance, if you're skiing in a national forest, register at the nearest ranger station. If you're skiing at a national park, register at the park headquarters.

Even if your route takes you through a commercial ski area, notify someone in authority before you leave. Usually this means informing the local ski patrol representative of your plans.

• Don't make the mistake of underestimating the time you're going to be on the trail. Deep snow or unbroken snow can slow your progress, so allow extra time for these. And remember that your expedition is never going to travel any faster than the slowest member of your party.

• Never ski on privately-owned land without first requesting permission.

• If you ski over remote farmland, beware of barbed wire fences. When a fence crosses your path, your best bet is to stop and remove your skis before trying to cross it.

Watch out for wire fences that may be hidden under the snow. Catch a tip on a strand of wire and a nasty spill can result.

Be careful on wooden foot bridges. You can catch a tip in a bridge plank.

• Be careful when crossing wooden foot bridges. You can get the tip of a ski pole stuck between bridge plants and snap it off.

• Early or late in the season, you may occasionally encounter small pools of water that have to be crossed. Only as a last resort should you consider wading through the water on skis, even if your boots are as waterproof as a duck's belly.

If it's possible, remove your skis and jump over the water. Or go around the pool, even if it means leaving the trail, removing

90

your skis, and making your way through thick brush.

Getting your skis wet when temperatures are below freezing and then placing them back on the snow, may cause them to ice up. You'll have to get out your scraper and go to work on them. It's a "headache."

• If you ski vigorously for very long, you'll begin to get thirsty. You may come upon a spring or a stream from which you can drink. If you're planning to stop and prepare a meal, you can always melt snow over a campfire or portable stove.

You can try carrying a canteen. But if the temperature starts heading toward zero, you'll find yourself hauling a block of ice. It's always wise to drink plenty of water before you start out.

THE BILL KOCH SKI LEAGUE

A 20-year-old, boyish-faced Vermonter astounded the world of sports in the 1976 Winter Olympics by winning a silver medal in the 30-kilometer race, a brutal test covering slightly more than 18 miles. The skier's name was Bill Koch (rhymes with poke).

Koch's stunning performance marked the first time that an American had captured an Olympic cross-country medal. Indeed, no American had even come close before him.

Koch comes from the town of Guilford, Vermont, and began skiing at the age of two. "My father had me sliding on wooden skis in my backyard by the time I could walk," he once said.

When he was six, Bill was ski jumping. Everyday he raced his classmates' bus to school on skis. Koch was once asked whether the bus always won. Grinning, he replied, "It depended on the snow conditions."

Koch won trophies as a jumper, then switched to cross-country skiing. Although he made rapid improvement, his career went almost unnoticed until his surprise performance in the 1976 Olympics.

In recognition of his achievement, the *U.S. Ski Association* organized the Bill Koch Ski League in 1978 for boys and girls, 13 years old and younger. You can join by yourself, or get together with some friends and an adult and form a Bill Koch Ski League in your area.

Some clubs sponsor regular cross-country outings. Others offer cross-country races.

To join, send a $1 membership fee to: U.S. Ski Association, Bill Koch Ski League, Box 777, Brattleboro, VT 05301.

You'll receive a poster that depicts Bill Koch skiing, a membership card, arm patch and newsletter.

Bill Koch Ski Leagues offer cross-country competition.

SKIING COMPETITION

Once you become skilled and experienced in cross-country skiing, you may want to compete against other skiers. There are more and more races and special events each year, sponsored by the U.S. Ski Association (USSA). For information on competition in your area, contact your regional USSA office:

Alaska—SRA Box 473-T, Anchorage, AK 99507.

Central—P.O. Box 66014, AMF O'Hare, Chicago, IL 60666.

Contestants line up for the start of the annual Nordic Holiday Race at Yosemite National Park, California.

Eastern—22 High St., Brattleboro, VT 05301.

Far West—3325 Wilshire Blvd., Suite 1340, Los Angeles, CA 90010.

Intermountain—1431 Terry Dr., Idaho Falls, ID 83401.

Northern—1732 Clark Ave., Billings, MT 59102.

Pacific Northwest—P.O. Box 6228, Seattle, WA 98188.

Rocky Mountain—1462 Larimer Sq., Denver, CO 80202.

Southern—Box 801, Belmont, NC 28012.

The address for the main office of the USSA is: 1726 Champa St., Suite 300, Denver, CO 80202.

Skiing in Canada is supervised by the Canadian Ski Association, 333 River Rd., Place Vanier, Tower A, Vanier City, ON K1L 8B9.

Lone cross-country racer hurries along against Rocky Mountains backdrop.

8 Where to Ski

You can ski in your backyard, of course, and in local parks or deserted golf courses. Forests and farmland offer other opportunities.

Besides these locations, there are countless ski areas that have been established just for the cross-country skier. They can be found in most parts of the United States and Canada.

These ski areas cover a wide range in what they offer. At some, you'll find only one or two trails and a ski-rental shop. At others, there are a dozen or more trails to choose from, varying in length and how difficult they may be. There are rentals shops, warming huts along the trails, instruction schools and clinics, lighted trails for nighttime skiing, and comfortable lodges for overnight guests.

It would be impossible to give the names of all the North American cross-country ski areas. The pages that follow list many of those that offer trails and other features suited for young skiers, beginner skiers.

The address for each area is also given. Write and inquire as to the number of trails and character of each.

Are they marked trails? That is, are they posted with directional signs? Or are they prepared trails? Are they laid out with tracks?

Also inquire as to what fees might be charged. Besides fees for renting equipment, there can be trail fees and instruction fees.

Many state parks offer opportunities for cross-country skiing. Write to the Division of Tourism at the state capital of the state in which you're interested. Ask for brochures describing the state's cross-country ski areas.

Finally, there are the national parks and national forests. Write to the forest or park in your region for information. The addresses for these are listed at the end of the section.

Also listed are the names of the principal guidebooks for cross-country skiing. These contain descriptions and maps of trails and tours in various parts of the United States and Canada. Some of the guidebooks are free.

EAST

Connecticut

Blackberry River Ski Touring
    Center
Route 44
Norfolk, CT 06058

Mohawk Mountain Ski Area
West Cornwall, CT 06796

Peoples State Forest
Connecticut Forest and Park
    Association
P.O. Box 389
East Hartford, CT 06108

Pine Mountain
Great World, Inc.
250 Farms Village Rd.
P.O. Box 250
W. Simsbury, CT 06092

Powder Ridge Ski Area
Middlefield, CT 06455

Riverrunning Touring Center
Main St.
Falls Village, CT 06031

White Memorial Foundation
Rt. 202
Litchfield, CT 06759

Woodbury Ski Area
Rt. 47
Woodbury, Ct 06798

Maine

Acadia National Park
Rt. 1
Bar Harbor, ME 04609

Akers Ski
Andover, ME 04216

The Birches Cross-Country
    Ski Area
Rockwood, ME 04478

Carrabasset Valley Recreation
    Center
Box 518
Carrabassett Valley, ME 04947

Deer Farm Ski Touring Center
Deer Farm Camps
Kingfield, ME 04947

Lost Valley
Lost Valley Rd.
Auburn, ME 04210

Pleasant Mountain
Mountain Rd.
Bridgeton, ME 04009

Squaw Mountain
Box D
Greenville, ME 04441

State of Maine Touring Center
Box 490
Rangeley, ME 04970

Sunday River Ski Touring
    Center

Sunday River Inn
Bethel, ME 04217

Maryland

Herrington Manor State Park
Rt. 5
Box 22
Oakland, MD 21550

New Germany State Park
Grantsville, MD 21536

Swallow Falls State Park
Oakland, MD 21550

Massachusetts

Butternut Ski Touring Center
Butter Basin
Route 23
Great Barrington, MA 01230

Cummington Farm Ski Touring
    Center
South Rd.
Cummington, MA 01026

Egremont Country Club Touring
    Center
Rt. 23
Great Barrington, MA 02130

Jug End Resort
South Egremont, MA 02158

Mt. Tom Ski Area
Holyoke, MA 01040

Nashoba Valley Ski Area
101 Hayward Rd.
Acton, MA 01720

Northfield Mountain Ski
   Touring Center
R.R. 1
Box 377
Northfield, MA 01360

Otis Ridge Ski Area
Rt. 23
Otis, MA 02153

Riverrun North
Rt. 7
Sheffield, MA 02157

New Hampshire

The Balsams
Dixville Notch, NH 03576

Bretton Woods Touring Center
Bretton Woods, NH 03575

Cannon Mountain
Franconia, NH 03580

Charmingfare Ski Touring
   Center
South Rd.
Candia, NH 03034

Dexter's Inn
Sunapee, NH 03782

Eastman Touring Center
Box 53
Grantham, NH 03753

Franconia Inn
Rt. 116
Franconia, NH 03580

Gray Ledges
Grantham, NH 03753

Gunstock
Box 366
Gilford, NH 03246

Jackson Ski Touring Foundation
Box 90F
Jackson, NH 03846

Loon Mountain
Lincoln, NH 03251

Moose Mountain Lodge
Elna, NH 03750

Mt. Sunapee Ski Area
Mt. Sunapee, NH 03722

The Nordic Skier
19 N. Main St.
Wolfboro, NH 03894

Norsk Ski Touring Center
Rt. 11
New London, NH 03257

Summers Mountain Ski Touring
   Center
Box F
Rt. 101
Dublin, NH 03444

Sunset Hill House
Sugar Hill, NH 03505

Temple Mountain Ski Touring
   Center
Rt. 101
Peterborough, NH 03458

Waterville Valley Ski Touring
   Center
Box 10
Waterville Valley, NH 03223

White Mountain Country Club

Cold Spring Properties
Ashland, NH 03217

Windblown
Turnpike Rd.
New Ipswich, NH 03701

New Jersey

Craigmeur Ski Area
Greenpond Rd.
Newfoundland, NJ 07435

Fairview Lake Ski Touring
Center
Fairview Lake Rd.
Stillwater, NJ 07875

Palisades Interstate Park
P.O. Box 155
Alpine, NJ 07620

Vernon Valley/Great Gorge
Box 848
McAfee, NJ 07428

New York

Adirondack Loj
Box 867
Lake Placid, NY 12946

Alpine Recreation Center
298 Ellicott Rd.
West Falls, NY 14170

Adirondack Ski Tours
Box 934
Saranac Lake, NY 12983

Bark Eater Ski Touring Center
Alstead Mill Rd.
Keene, NY 12942

Bear Mountain Cross Country
Skiing
Palisades Interstate Park
Commission
Bear Mountain, NY 10911

Belleayre Mt. Ski Center
Pine Hill, NY 12465

Beresford Farms Ski Touring
Center
RD 1
Delanson, NY 12053

Big Tupper
Box 820
Tupper Lake, NY 12986

Cascade Ski Touring Center
Box 190
Lake Placid, NY 12946

Clover Reach Ski Trails
West Ghent, NY 12075

Country Hills Farms
North Rd.
Tully, NY 13159

Erie Bridge Inn
RD 2
Camden, NY 13316

Garnet Hill Ski Touring Center
North River, NY 12856

Glens Falls Ski Touring Center
Recreation Department
Ridge St.
Glens Falls, NY 12801

Gore Mountain Ski Center
North Creek, NY 12853

Hanson's Trail North
895 New Loudon Rd.
Latham, NY 12110

Indian Lake Village
Indian Lake, NY 12842

Inlet Ski Touring Center
Old Forge, NY 13420

Lake Placid Resort Hotel
Lake Placid, NY 12946

Mohonk Mountain House
Lake Mohonk
New Paltz, NY 12561

Mt. Van Hoevenberg Recreation
    Area
New York State Dept. of
    Environmental Conservation
50 Wolf Rd.
Albany, NY 12233

Ninety Acres Ski Center
8012 East Genessee St.
Fayetteville, NY 13066

The Nordic Way
Colden Langlauf Trails
8356 Center St.
Holland, NY 14080

Paleface Ski Center
Rt. 86
P.O. Box 163
Jay, NY 12941

Pechler's Trails Ski Touring
    Center
Shilling Rd.
Palmyra, NY 14522

Podunk Cross Country Ski
    Center
Podunk Rd.
Trumansburg, NY 14886

Saratoga Mountain Ski Touring
    Center
Saratoga Spa State Park
Saratoga Springs, NY 12866

Skaneateles Ski Touring Center
Rt. 20
Village East Line
Skaneateles, NY 13152

Snow Ridge
Turin, NY 13473

Sojourn Farm Ski Touring
    Center
RD 1
Cayuga, NY 13034

Star Lake Campus
State University
Potsdam, NY 13676

Swain Ski School
Swain, NY 14884

Ward Pound Ridge Reservation
Cross River, NY 10518

White Birches Ski Touring
    Center
Windham, NY 12496

Williams Lake Hotel
Rosendale, NY 12472

Wills Run
Hoffman Rd.
Schroon Lake, NY 12870

North Carolina

Nantahala Outdoor Center
Star Route
Box 68
Bryson City, NC 28713

Pennsylvania

Apple Valley Ski Area
RD 1
Zionsville, PA 18092

Blue Knob Resort
Box 344
Claysburg, PA 16625

Crystal Lake Camps
RD 1
Hughesville, PA 17737

Hidden Valley Ski Area
RD 4
Somerset, PA 15501

Pocono 500 Ski Lodge
Reeders, PA 18352

Starlight Lake
Starlight, PA 18461

Tanglewood Ski Area
Rt. 390
Lake Wallenpaupack
Tafton, PA 18464

Tiadaghton State Forest
Pennsylvania Bureau of Forestry
423 East Central Ave.
South Williamsport, PA 17701

Vermont

Blueberry Hill Cross Country
Ski Center
Goshen, VT 05733

Bolton Valley Resort
Bolton, VT 05477

Burke Mountain Touring Center
East Burke, VT 05832

Burklyn Ski Touring Center
East Burke, VT 05832

Churchill House Touring Center
RFD 3
Brandon, VT 05733

Cortina Inn
Killington, VT 05751

Edson Hill Ski Touring Center
RR 1
Edson Hill
Stowe, VT 05672

Grafton Cross-Country Trail
System
Grafton, VT 05146

Green Mountain Ski Touring
Center
Green Mountain Stock Farm
Randolph, VT 05060

Green Trails Ski Touring Center
By the Floating Bridge
Brookfield, VT 05036

Hazen's Notch Ski Touring
Center
Rt. 58
Montgomery Center, VT 05471

Highland Lodge Ski Touring
Greensboro, VT 05841

Mt. Ascutney Ski Area
Rt. 44
Brownsville, VT 05037

Mt. Mansfield Company
Stowe, VT 05672

Mt. Snow Alpine Ski Area
Mt. Snow, VT 05356

Mountain Meadows Ski Touring
   Center
50 Thundering Brook Rd.
Killington, VT 05751

Mountain Top Ski Touring
   Center
Chittenden, VT 05737

Nordic Inn Ski Touring Center
Rt. 11
Landgrove, VT 05148

Okemo Mountain
RFD 1
Ludlow, VT 05149

Ole's Cross-Country Center
Warren, VT 05674

Rabbit Hill Inn Ski
Touring Center
Lower Waterford, VT 05848

Ski Tours of Vermont
RFD 1
Chester, VT 05143

Smuggler's Notch Ski Area
Jeffersonville, VT 05464

Snow Valley Ski Touring Center
Londonderry, VT 05148

Stratton Ski Touring Center
Stratton Mountain, VT 05155

Sunshine Ski Touring Center
Rt. 242
Jay, VT 05859

Topnotch at Stowe
Mountain Rd.
Stowe, VT 05672

Snow Valley Ski Touring Center
Londonderry, VT 05148

Trapp Family Lodge Ski
   Touring Center
Stowe, VT 05672

Viking Ski Touring Centre
Little Pond Rd.
Londonderry, VT 05148

Wild Wings Ski Touring Center
Box 132
Peru, VT 05152

Woodstock Ski Touring Center
Woodstock, VT 05091

Virginia

Mt. Rogers Recreation Area
Appalachian Outfitters
Box 7A
Salem, VA 24153

West Virginia

Monongahela National Forest
Box 110
Richwood, WV 26261

Snowshoe Ski Touring Area
Slatyfork, WV 26291

Illinois

Cook County Forest Preserves
536 N. Harlem Ave.
River Forest, IL 60305

Galena Territory
Box 1000
Galena, IL 61036

Moraine Hills State Park
914 S. River Rd.
McHenry, IL 60050

Indiana

Dunes State Park
Box 322
Chesterton, IN 46304

Pokagon State Park
R.R. 2
Box 29C
Angola, IN 46703

Potato State Recreation Area
65601 Pine Rd.
North Liberty, IN 46554

Iowa

Stephens State Forest
State Conservation Commission
Wallace State Office Building
Des Moines, IA 50319

Yellow River State Forest
State Conservation Commission
Wallace State Office Building
Des Moines, IA 50319

Michigan

Bintz Apple Mountain Ski Shop
4535 N. River Rd.
Freeland, MI 48623

Boyne Highlands Cross Country
Skiing
Harbor Springs, MI 49740

Boyne Mountain Cross Country
Skiing
Boyne Falls, MI 49713

Champion Nordic Ski Area
North M-95
Champion, MI 49814

Cross-Country Ski Headquarters
Higgins Lake, MI 48653

Greenwood Campground
West Greenwood Rd.
Alger, MI 48610

Hanson Recreation Area
P.O. Box 361
Grayling, MI 49738

Hilton Shanty Creek
Box 355
Bellaire, MI 49615

Hinchman Acres Resort
Box 146
Mio, MI 48647

Lake Doster
135 Golf View Dr.
Plainwell, MI 49080

Lost Lake Resort
Paradise, MI 49768

Porcupine Mountains State Park
Ontonagon, MI 49953

Ranch Rudolf
P.O. Box 587
Traverse City, MI 49684

Schuss Mountain
Mancelona, MI 49659

Sharoco Farm
Savage and Baldhill Rds.
Jones, MI 49061

Sky Valley Ranch
Box 11
Kalkaska, MI 49646

Sugar Loaf Mountain Resort
RR 1
Cedar, MI 49621

Suicide Bowl
Ishpeming Chamber of
    Commerce
201 E. Division St.
Ishpeming, MI 49849

Sylvania Wilderness Area
Sylvania Outfitters
West U.S. 2
Watersmeet, MI 49969

Tahquamenon Falls State Park
Paradise, MI 48768

Minnesota

Eagle Mountain Ski Area
Box 98
Grey Eagle, MN 56336

Hennepin County Parks
c/o Hyland Lake Park Reserve
Box 32
Maple Plain, MI 55359

Lutsen Ski Area
Box 86
Lutsen, MN 55612

Manitou Lakes Cross-Country
    Ski Trails
42nd Ave. N.
Minneapolis, MN 55427

National Forest Lodge
Isabella, MN 55607

Quadna Mountain
Hill City, MN 55748

Radisson Inn
Grand Portage, MN 55605

Savanna State Forest
McGregor, MN 55760

Ski Touring Centers
Minneapolis Park & Recreation
    Board
240 S. 4th St.
Minneapolis, MN 55415

Spirit Mountain
9500 Spirit Mountain Pl.
Duluth, MN 55810

Sugar Hills
Box 369
Grand Rapids, MN 55744

Val Chatel
Park Rapids, MN 56470

104

Ohio

Ohio Department of Natural
    Resources
Division of Parks & Recreation
Fountain Square
Columbus, OH 43244

Towner's Woods
Portage County Park &
    Recreation Department
449 S. Meridian
Ravenna, OH 44266

Wisconsin

Anvil Lake Trails
Russell's Resort
Route 3
Eagle River, WI 54521

Black River State Forest
Rt. 4
Box 5
Black River Falls, WI 54615

Blackhawk Ridge
Box 92
Sauk City, WI 53583

Chanticleer Inn
Rt. 3
Eagle River, WI 54521

Chequamegon National Forest
P.O. Box 280
Park Falls, WI 54552

Consolidated Trails
P.O. Box 50
Wisconsin Rapids, WI 54494

Copper Falls State Park
Ashland, WI 54806

Door County Touring Center
Box 219
Sturgeon Bay, WI 54235

Eagle River Nordic Ski Center
P.O. Box 936
Eagle River, WI 54521

Egg Harbor Lodge
P.O. Box 57
Egg Harbor, WI 54209

The Farm
Box 191
Brentwood, WI 54513

Fox Hills Inn
Box 129
Mishicot, WI 54228

Gerbick Lake Trails
Route 5
Tomahawk, WI 55487

Greenbush Ski Area
Box 426
Campbellsport, WI 53010

Hardscrabble Cross-Country Ski
    Area
Rice Lake, WI 54868

Hoofbeat Ridge
Rt. 2
Mazomanie, WI 53560

Kemos Ski Trail
70 North Jackson St.
Hartford, WI 53027

Mt. La Crosse
La Crosse, WI 54601

Newman Springs Trail
P.O. Box 280
Park Falls, WI 54552

Newport State Park
Ellison Bay, WI 54210

Olympia Resort
1350 Royale Mile Rd.
Oconomowoc, WI 53066

Olympia Sport Village
Box 3
Upson, WI 54565

Omnibus Nordic Ski Center
Fish Creek, WI 54212

Otter Run Trails
Merrill, WI 54452

Peninsula State Park
Fish Creek, WI 54212

Pike Lake State Park
70 N. Johnson St.
Hartford, WI 53027

Port Mountain
Box 840
Bayfield, WI 54814

Telemark Lodge
Cable, WI 54821

Thunder Lake Ski Touring
  Center
Box 215
Rt. 2
Eagle River, WI 54521

Timberlake Lodge
Rt. 2
Turtle Lake, WI 54889

Trees for Tomorrow
  Environmental Center
P.O. Box 609
Eagle River, WI 54521

Underdown Wilderness Area
Merrill, WI 54452

Whitecap Mountain Ski Area
Montreal, WI 54550

Wildcat Mountain State Park
Box 98
Ontario, WI 54651

The Wintergreen
P.O. Box 467
Spring Green, WI 53588

Wolf River Lodge
White Lake, WI 54491

Woodside Ranch Resort
Mauston, WI 53948

PACIFIC COAST

Alaska

Alyeska Resort
P.O. Box 249

Girdwood, AK 99587

Birch Hill Ski Area
c/o Fairbanks Chamber of
  Commerce

Fairbanks, AK 97701

Nordic Ski Club of Anchorage
Box 3301
Anchorage, AK 99501

Nordic Ski Club of Fairbanks
College, AK 99701

University of Alaska Trails
　System
Physical Education Department
University of Alaska
Fairbanks, AK 99701

California

Bear Valley Nordic Ski School
Box 5
Bear Valley, CA 95223

Big Chief Guides
Box 2427
Truckee, CA 95734

Childs Meadows Nordic Ski
　Area
P.O. Box 2
Mill Creek, CA 96061

Ebbetts Pass Ski Touring Center
Tamarack Lodge
P.O. Box 56
Bear Valley, CA 95223

Lassen National Park
Mineral, CA 96063

Mammoth Ski Touring Center
P.O. Box 102
Mammoth Lakes, CA 93546

Northstar Nordic Ski Center
P.O. Box 129

Truckee, CA 95734

Royal Gorge Nordic Ski Resort
P.O. Box 178
Soda Springs, CA 95728

Sequoia Ski Touring
Sequoia National Park, CA
　93262

Squaw Valley Nordic Center
Box 2288
Olympic Valley, CA 95730

Sugar House West
Meyers, CA 95705

Tahoe City Nordic Ski Center
Box 1632
Tahoe City, CA 95730

Yosemite Mountaineering School
Yosemite National Park
Yosemite, CA 95389

Oregon

Mt. Bachelor Nordic Sports
　Center
P.O. Box 828
Bend, OR 97701

Odell Lake Lodge
P.O. Box 72
Crescent Lake, OR 97425

Sunriver Nordic Ski Center
Sunriver, OR 97701

Telemark Cross-Country Ski
　School
3735 N.E. Shaver St.
Portland, OR 97212

Timberline Lodge
Government Camp, OR 97028

Washington

Adventure Chalet
P.O. Box 312
Leavenworth, WA 98826

Batnuni Lake Resort
1628 Ninth Ave.
Seattle, WA 98101

The Cross-Country Center

P.O. Box 118
Snoqualmie Pass, WA 98068

Mt. Ranier National Park
Tahoma Woods
Star Route
Ashford, WA 98304

Mountainholm
2126 Westlake Ave.
Seattle, WA 98121

Sun Mountain
P.O. Box 1000
Winthrop, WA 98862

West

Arizona

Apache National Forest
c/o Greer Chamber of
    Commerce
P.O. Box 121
Greer, AZ 85927

Mormon Lake Ski Touring
    Center
Mormon Lake, AZ 86038

Sacred Mountain Ski Tours
406 S. Beaver St.
Flagstaff, AZ 86001

Colorado

Ashcroft Ski Touring Unlimited
Box 1572
Aspen, CO 81611

Bear Pole Ranch
Star Route 1
Steamboat Springs, CO 80477

Breckenridge Ski Touring School
P.O. Box 1058
Breckenridge, CO 80424

C Lazy U Ranch
Box 378
Granby, CO 80446

Copper Mountain Ski Escape
    Touring Center
Box 1
Copper Mountain, CO 80443

Devil's Thumb Cross Country
    Ski Center
Box 125
Fraser, CO 80442

Durango Colorado Nordic
Chamber of Commerce
Durango, CO 81301

Fothergill's Outdoor Sportsman
Box 88
Aspen, CO 81611

Glen Eden Ranch
Box 867
Clark, CO 80428

Keystone Touring Center
Box 38
Keystone, CO 80435

Lake Eldora Ski Area
Box 430
Nederland, CO 80466

Mountaincraft Tours
Box 359
Steamboat Springs, CO 80477

Nordic Adventure Ski Touring
    Center
Box 528
Crested Butte, CO 81224

Peaceful Valley Ski Touring
    Center
Star Route
Lyons, CO 80540

Rocky Mountain Ski Tours
P.O. Box 413
Estes Park, CO 80517

Scandinavian Lodge
P.O. Box 5040
Steamboat Springs, CO 80499

Snow Mountain Ranch YMCA
Box 558
Granby, CO 80446

Snowmass Ski Touring Center
Snowmass Village, CO 81615

Steamboat Springs Ski Touring
    Center
Box 1178
Steamboat Springs, CO 80477

Tour Idlewild
Box 1
Hideaway Park, CO 80450

Vail Ski Touring School
Box 811
Vail, CO 81657

Vista Verde Guest Ranch
Box 465
Steamboat Springs, CO 80477

Idaho

Craters of the Moon National
    Monument
Box 29
Arco, ID 83213

Galena Lodge Ski Touring
    Center
Star Route
Ketchum, ID 83340

Sawtooth Mountaineering
Main St.
Idaho City, ID 83704

Sun Valley Ski Touring Center
Box 272
Sun Valley, ID 83353

Montana

Big Sky of Montana
P.O. Box 1
Big Sky, MT 59716

Glacier National Park
West Glacier, MT 59936

Northern Nordic Ski Center
232 Central Ave.
Whitefish, MT 59937

Whitefish Nordic Ski Center
139 2nd St.
Whitefish, MT 59937

Woody Creek Cross-Country
    Center
Box 1044
Cooke City, MT 59020

Yellowstone Nordic Ski Center
Box 488
West Yellowstone, MT 59758

North Dakota

North Dakota Parks and
    Recreation Department
Route 2
Box 139
Mandan, ND 58554

South Dakota

Deer Mountain
Box 622
Deadwood, SD 57732

Terry Peak
136 Sherman St.
Deadwood, SD 57732

Utah

Brian Head Nordic Ski Center
Box 30
Brian Head, UT 84719

Brighton Ski Bowl
Brighton, UT 84121

Bryce Canyon National
    Monument

Box 747
Cedar City, UT 84720

Snow Basin
Ogden, UT 84404

Snowbird Cross-Country Center
Snowbird, UT 84070

White Pine Ski Touring Center
Box 417
Park City, UT 84060

Wyoming

Cache Creek
Bridger-Teton National Forest
Box 1689
Jackson, WY 83001

Flagg Ranch Village
P.O. Box 187
Moran, WY 83013

Grand Targhee Cross-Country
    Ski School
Alta, Wyoming, via Driggs, ID
83422

Grant Teton National Park
Box 170
Moose, WY 83012

Jackson Hole Nordic Ski Center
Box 1226
Jackson, WY 83001

Old Faithful Snowlodge
Yellowstone National Park
Yellowstone, WY 82190

Powderhead Ski Tours
Box 286

Wilson, WY 83014

Snow King Cross-Country Ski
  School

Box 427

Jackson, WY 83001

CANADA

Alberta

Banff National Park
Box 1298
Banff, AB T0L 0C0

Jasper National Park
Box 10
Jasper, AB T0E 1E0

Kananaskis Valley Touring
  Center
Kananaskis Provincial Park
Seebe, AB T0L 1X0

Maligne Lake
Box 280
Jasper, AB T0E 1E0

Marmot Basin
Box 472
Jasper, AB T0E 1E0

Sunshine Village Nordic Center
Box 1510
Banff, AB T0L 0C0

British Columbia

Bowron Lake Provincial Park
Box 33
Barkerville, BC V0K 1B0

Crooked River Provincial Park
Box 2045
Prince George, BC V2N 2J6

Cypress Provincial Park
1600 Indian River Dr., North
Vancouver, BC 47G 1L3

Kitimat Cross-Country Skiing
82 Clifford St.
Kitimat, BC V8C 1B4

Manning Provincial Park
Manning Park, BC V0X 1R0

Mt. Revelstoke National Park
Box 350
Revelstoke, BC V0E 2S0

Mt. Seymour Provincial Park
1600 Indian River Dr.
North Vancouver, BC V7G 1L3

108 Resort Ranch
RR 1
100 Mile House, BC V0K 2E0

Red Coach Inn
P.O. Box 760
100 Mile House, BC V0K 2E0

Ten Mile Lake Provincial Park
Barkerville, BC V0K 1B0

Whistler Ski Area
Box 96
Whistler, BC V0N 1B0

Manitoba

Canadian Ski Association

111

Manitoba Division
1301 Ellice Ave.
Winnipeg, MB R3C 1T5

New Brunswick

Kouchibouguac National Park
Kent Count NB E0A 2A0

Mactaquac Ski Touring
c/o Division of Tourism
Province of New Brunswick
Box 1345
Fredericton, NB E3B 5C3

Silver Winter Park
c/o Wostawea Ski Club
RR 4
Fredericton, NB E3B 4R7

Sugar Loaf Ski Touring
c/o Department of Tourism
Province of New Brunswick
Box 12345
Fredericton, NB E3B 5C3

Newfoundland

Gros Morne National Park
P.O. Box 130
Rocky Harbor, NF A0K 4N0

Nova Scotia

Canadian Hosteling Association
Maritime Region
P.O. Box 3010
Halifax, NS B3J 3G6

Nakkertok Ski Touring Area
c/o Canadian Ski Association

2375 Cheshire Rd.
Ottawa, ON K2C 1G2

Nangor Cross Country Resort
Westmeath, ON K0J 2L0

Ontario

Albion Hills Ski Center
5 Shoreham Dr.
Downsview, ON M3N 1S4

Bear Trail Inn Resort
Whitnet, ON K0J 2M0

Blue Mountain Resorts
RR 3
Collingwood, ON L9Y 3Z2

Hidden Valley Highlands Ski
 Club
P.O. Box 74
RR 2
Huntsville, ON P0A 1K0

Horseshoe Valley Resort
Box 607
Barrie, ON L4M 4V1

Molson's Park Touring Center
1 Big Bay Point Rd.
Barrie, ON L4N 4T2

Mountain View Ski Area
RR 2
Midland, ON L4R 4K4

Nordic Inn
P.O. Box 155
Dorset, ON P0A 1E0

Senaca King
Senaca College
Dufferin St., N.

RR 3
King City, ON L0G 1K0

Shanty Bay Cross Country Ski
    Resort
Shanty Bay, ON L0L 2L0

Ski Haven Country Club
RR 1
Gilford, ON L0L 1R0

Talisman Resort Hotel
Kimberley, ON 1G0

Prince Edward Island

Prince Edward Island National
    Park
Box 487
Charlottetown, PE C1A 7L1

Quebec

Alpine Inn
Ste. Marguerite Station, PQ
J0T 1K0

Auberge Normande
C.P. 723
Lake Beauport, PQ G0A 2C0

Camp Fortune
Old Chelsea, PQ J0X 2N0

Des Voltgeurs Park
P.O. Box 878
Drummondville, PQ J2B 6X1

Far Hills Inn
Val Morin Station, PQ J0T 2S0

Laurentides Park
Cyrille St., East
P.O. Box 8888
Quebec City, PQ G1K 7W3

Le Chantecler Ski Resort
Ste. Adele, PQ J0R 1L0

L'Esterel
Ville D'Esterel
Prevost, PQ J0T 1E0

Mont Orford Park
P.O. Box 146
Magog, PQ J1X 3W7

Mont St. Bruno Park
2265 de la Province
Longueil, PQ J4G 1G3

Mont Ste. Anne Park
P.O. Box 400
Beaupre, PQ G0A 1E0

Mont Tremblant Park
Lac Superieur, PQ J0T 1P0

Villa Bellevue
Mont Tremblant, PQ J0T 1Z0

Saskatchewan

Sasketchewan Department of
    Tourism
Government Administration
    Building
Regina, SK S4S 0B1

Saskatchewan Ski Association
Cross Country Discipline
26 Porteus Crescent
Sakatoon, SK S7J 2S8

GUIDEBOOKS FOR
CROSS-COUNTRY SKIING

East

Ski Touring Guide and Directory (brochure, no charge) Ski Touring Operators' Association, Bretton Woods, NH 03575. Describes New England cross-country areas and pinpoints them on a map.

Ski Touring in New England and New York, Lance Tapley, 1976, 192 pages ($4.95). Stone Wall Press, 5 Byron St., Boston, MA 02108. Tour descriptions plus instructional advice. Also a brief history of the sport.

Midwest

Michigan Cross-Country Skiing, Dennis R. Hansen, 1977, 131 pages ($4.95). Hansen Publishing Co., P.O. Box 1723, East Lansing, MI 48823. Descriptions and maps of areas.

Sourcebook of Ski Touring, 1978-79 edition, 40 pages ($2). U.S. Ski Association, Central Division, P.O. Box 66014, Chicago, IL 60666. A guide to areas in the Midwest, plus instructional advise and safety tips.

Wisconsin Cross Country Skiing (pamphlet; no charge), State Division of Tourism, P.O. Box 7606, Madison, WI 53707.

West

A Guide to Cross-Country Ski Tours at Lake Tahoe, Skip Reedy, 1979. ($3.50). Tahoe Ski Center, Box 1632, Tahoe City, CA 95730.

Central Colorado Ski Tours, Tom and Sanse Suddoth, 1977, 140 pages ($5.95). Pruett Publishing Co., 3235 Prairie Ave., Boulder, CO 80301. Descriptions of 58 tours.

Colorado Front Range Tours, Tom and Sanse Suddoth, 1975, 128 pages ($5.95). Touchstone Press, P.O. Box 81, Beaverton, OR 97005. Descriptions of tours in Boulder and Denver areas.

Northern Colorado Ski Tours, Tom and Sanse Suddoth, 1976, 141 pages ($5.95). Touchstone Press, P.O. Box 81, Beaverton, OR 97005. Descriptions of 65 tours.

Oregon Ski Tours, Doug and Sally Sharrad, 1973, 160 pages ($6.95). Touchstone Press, P.O. Box 81, Beaverton, OR 97005.

Snow Tours in Western Washington, Randy McDougall, editor, 1976, 96 pages ($2.50). Singpost, 16812 36th Ave. W., Lynnwood, WA 98036.

Canada

British Columbia Cross Country Ski Routes, Rochelle and Richard Wright, 1976, 80 pages ($3.95). Antonson Publishing Co., 12165 97th Ave., Surrey, BC V3V 2C8.

Cross-Country Ski Trails in the Laurentians, ($2). La Zone De Ski Laurentienne, 306 A Place De Youville, Montreal, PQ H2Y 2B6.

Cross-Country Skiing and Snowshoeing in Quebec, 38 pages (no charge). Ministry of Tourism, Government of Quebec, 150 E. St., Cyrille Blvd., PQ G1R 4Y1.

Cross Country Skiing in Ontario, Iris Nowell, 1978, 80 pages ($2.95). Greey De Pencier, 59 Front St. E., Toronto, ON M5E 1B3. Descriptive information and maps.

Ski Trails in the Canadian Rockies, Rich Kunelius, 138 pages ($4.95).

Summerthought, Ltd., P.O. Box 1420, Banff, AB T0L 0C0. Guide to parks plus survival information.

The White Book of U.S. Ski Areas, 410 pages ($7.95). Inter-Ski Services, Box 3635 Georgetown Station, Washington, D.C. 20007. A directory covering all ski areas in the United States and Canada.

U.S. FOREST SERVICE
REGIONAL OFFICES

Alaska Region
Federal Office Building
P.O. Box 1628
Juneau, AK 99801

California Region
630 Sansome St.
San Francisco, CA 94111

Eastern Region
633 West Wisconsin Ave.
Milwaukee, WI 53203

Intermountain Region
324 25th St.
Ogden, UT 84401

Northern Region
Federal Building

Missoula, MT 59807

Pacific Northwest Region
319 S.W. Pine St.
P.O. Box 3623
Portland, OR 97208

Rocky Mountain Region
11177 W. 8th Ave.
P.O. Box 25127
Lakewood, CO 80225

Southern Region
1720 Peachtree Rd., N.W.
Atlanta, GA 30309

Southwestern Region
517 Gold Ave., S.W.
Albuquerque, NM 87102

NATIONAL PARK SERVICE
REGIONAL OFFICES

Mid-Atlantic Regional Office
143 South Third St.
Philadelphia, PA 19106

Midwest Regional Office
1709 Jackson St.
Omaha, NE 68102

National Capital Regional

Office
1100 Ohio Dr., S.W.
Washington, DC 20242

North Atlantic Regional
Office
150 Causeway St.
Boston, MA 02114

117

Pacific Northwest Regional
Office
Rm. 931
Fourth and Pike Bldg.
1424 Fourth Ave.
Seattle, WA 98101

Rocky Mountain Regional
Office
P.O. Box 25287
Denver, CO 80225

Southeast Regional Office
1895 Phoenix Blvd.
Atlanta, GA 30349

Southwest Regional Office
Old Santa Fe Trail
P.O. Box 728
Santa Fe, NM 87501

Western Regional Office
450 Golden Gate Ave.
Box 36063
San Francisco, CA 94102

Glossary

Alpine—Of or relating to downhill skiing.

backpack—A hiking pack made of nylon or canvas that is carried on the back and used to hold equipment or food.

base—A foundation of packed snow; also, a wax that is applied to the surface of cross-country skis to protect from moisture and wear.

basket—The webbed ring around the ski pole about four to six inches above the tip which is tied to the pole by straps, and which serves to keep the pole from sinking too deeply into the snow.

binder—A wax that is sometimes applied between the base wax and running waxes.

boat-cut—A type of cross-country racing ski in which the waist is wider than the tip or tail sections. A boat-cut ski is said to create less drag.

camber—The upward curve of a ski when viewed from the side from one end to the other. Camber is what makes a ski springy and helps distribute the skier's weight over the entire length of the ski.

Canadian Ski Association—The governing body of amateur skiing in Canada.

double-poling—To move oneself forward by pushing off with both poles at the same time.

gaiters—Leather or cloth coverings for the ankle, instep, and sometimes the lower leg. Gaiters prevent snow from getting inside one's boots.

herringbone—A method of climbing a hill which consists of taking alternate steps forward while keeping the tips of the skis pointed outward and the tails close together.

hypothermia—The reduction of body temperature through prolonged exposure to the cold.

inside—The side of the skier's body toward which a turn is being made (as in *inside* ski, *inside* knee, etc.).

kick—A striding motion in which the skier pushes decisively from one ski and glides on the other.

klister—A sticky running wax used when skiing temperatures are above freezing and the snow is wet.

mountaineering—Climbing high, snow-covered mountains on skis.

National Ski Patrol System—An organization of approximately 25,000 members with representatives at ski areas throughout the United States. The NSPS was established to promote ski safety and assist in the handling of injured skiers at ski areas.

Nordic skiing—Cross-country skiing.

off-track skiing—Skiing across open countryside. (Compared to track skiing.)

outside—The side of the skier's body away from the direction of the turn (as in *outside* ski, *outside* knee, etc.).

parallel cut—A ski that is the same width from tip to tail.

plane—To glide over the snow.

plowing—Making a deep furrow or groove in the snow.

powder—Light, fluffy, usually newly-fallen snow.

rucksack—A large backpack with outside pockets that rides high on the shoulders.

running wax—A wax that is applied to the bottom of some cross-country skis that is capable of holding the ski in position when it is placed down, but also permits the ski to slide forward, to glide.

shovel—The widest part of the ski near the tip.

sidecut—Term used to describe a cross-country ski that is wider at the tip and tail than in the middle.

sidestep—A method of climbing a slope by pointing the skis across the slope and stepping up sideways with the uphill ski and then bringing the downhill ski up to it. The process is repeated until the top of the slope is reached.

skating turn—An advanced method of turning in which one ski is thrust in the direction of the turn, and the skier quickly shifts his weight to it, then brings the other ski parallel to the first.

snowplow stop—A method of slowing down or stopping in which the tails of the skis are thrust outward and the tips brought together.

snowplow turn—A method of turning in from the snowplow position; one ski is weighted, causing a change of direction to the opposite side.

step turn—A method of changing direction by lifting one ski and swinging it out to the side in the direction of the turn, weighting it, and then bringing the other ski alongside.

tail—The rear part of the ski.

tip—The pointed front part of a ski.

tonkin—A type of cane or bamboo used in ski poles.

tour skiing, touring—Cross-country skiing.

track skiing—Cross-country skiing on a pair of parallel paths cut in the snow. Each path is several inches deep and slightly wider than a ski. (Compare to off-track skiing.)

tuque—A loosely-knitted stocking cap, traditionally worn by cross-country skiers.

United States Ski Association (USSA)—The governing body of amateur skiing in the United States.

wagon wheel. *See* step turn.

waist—The mid-portion of a ski.

waxless ski—A fiberglass ski in which a section of the bottom beneath the binding is rough-textured so as to enable the ski to grip when the skier strides forward.

weight—To shift the body's weight to a particular ski in traversing or turning.

wind-chill factor—The day's temperature as adjusted to take into account the velocity of the wind.

Index